CW00498157

THE TRAUMA
OF BIRTH

By Otto Rank

Martino Publishing
Mansfield Centre, CT
2010

Martino Publishing
P.O. Box 373,
Mansfield Centre, CT 06250 USA

www.martinopublishing.com

ISBN 1-57898-976-0

© *2010 Martino Publishing*

Cover design by T. Matarazzo

Printed in the United States of America On 100% Acid-Free Paper

THE TRAUMA
OF BIRTH

By Otto Rank

ROBERT BRUNNER

New York 1952

ROBERT BRUNNER
1212 AVENUE OF THE AMERICAS, NEW YORK 36, N.Y.

MANUFACTURED IN THE UNITED STATES OF AMERICA

THERE is an old story that King Midas had hunted for the wise Silenus, the companion of Dionysus, for a long time in the woods without catching him. But when he finally fell into his hands, the King asked: " What is the very best and the most preferable thing for Man ?" The demon remained silent, stubborn, and motionless; until he was finally compelled by the King, and then broke out into shrill laughter, uttering these words: " Miserable, ephemeral species, children of chance and of hardship, why do you compel me to tell you what is most profitable for you not to hear ? The very best is quite unattainable for you: it is, not to be born, not to exist, to be Nothing. But the next best for you is—to die soon."

NIETZSCHE : *The Birth of Tragedy.*

CONTENTS

TEXT ILLUSTRATIONS

PREFACE

THE following arguments indicate a first attempt to apply the psychoanalytic way of thinking, as such, to the comprehension of the whole development of mankind, even of the actual fact of becoming human. It would be more correct not to use the word " apply," for it is not a question of one of the usual works on the " Application of Psychoanalysis to the Mental Sciences "; rather it is a matter of making psychoanalytic thought productive for our entire conception of mankind and history. This finally represents the history of mind, that is, the history of the development of the human mind and of the things created by it.

This particular viewpoint, still too new to be quite clearly grasped, is made accessible to us through Psychoanalysis by reason of the prodigious extension of our consciousness, which at the present time enables us to recognize part of the deepest Unconscious as such, and to understand its mode of operation. As scientific knowledge itself is no more than a conscious comprehension of previously latent facts, it is only logical that every particle of the extension of our consciousness, gained by analysis, should be converted into understanding. It is now shown at a quite definite point of psychoanalytic knowledge, which we shall soon characterize more definitely, that there is also a considerable part of organic or biological development which can be understood only from the psychical side; that is, from the side which, together with all the residue of development, includes also our own instrument of knowledge, which has suddenly become definitely more efficient through our progressive knowledge of the Unconscious.

We have taken certain new individual psychoanalytic experiences solely as a starting-point for a more comprehensive view and for general knowledge; but we believe that in so doing we have opened up the way to something essentially different from the hitherto prevailing " application " of Psychoanalysis. Thus we also lay stress on the fact that we want to keep ourselves free from an overestimation of the psychoanalytic doctrine of the Unconscious as applied to therapy, without thereby departing from the psychoanalytic way of thinking. But at the same time we extend this line of thought in both directions. It is, then, no accident that Psychoanalysis, as soon as it began to develop from a therapeutic procedure into a doctrine of the Unconscious, almost simultaneously deviating from its original medical field, invaded and enriched wellnigh every mental science, and finally itself became one of the most important of mental movements of the present day. The psychic patient, from whose material and by whose help Psychoanalysis was discovered and developed, will always remain the native source for further investigation and extension of the doctrine. Yet this origin is of no more importance today than, for instance, the country from which Columbus set forth, and which furnished the bold explorer with practical means for his voyage.

We have attempted in the first place to sketch in the following pages a part of the further development of psychoanalysis itself, as it has proceeded from the consistent application of the method created by Freud, and from the doctrine based on the method. Then, starting from this basis, we have tried to gain a general and a wider knowledge through a direct comprehension of the Unconscious. Whoever is familiar with the particular course of psychoanalytic investigation will not be astonished to find that starting both generally and in individual cases from the upper layers of consciousness, and penetrating ever further into its hidden depths, this method ultimately reaches a point at which it finds its natural limitation, but likewise also its foundation. After a thorough examination of the Unconscious, its psychical content and complicated mechanism of conversion into the conscious, by the analysis both of abnormal and of normal people, we have come up against the final origin of the psychical unconscious in the psycho-physical, which we can now make biologically comprehensible as well. In attempting to reconstruct for the first time from analytic experiences the to all appearances purely physical birth trauma with its prodigious psychical consequences for the whole development of mankind, we are led to recognize in the birth trauma the ultimate biological basis of the psychical. In this way we gain a fundamental insight into the nucleus of the Unconscious on which Freud has constructed which may claim to be comprehensive and scientific. In this sense, the following arguments are only possible and intelligible on the basis of the whole body of knowledge gained

psychoanalytically, about the construction and the functioning of our own psychical instrument.

If it has thus become possible to give a biological basis to
the Unconscious, that is, to the psychical proper, discovered
and investigated by Freud, then a second purpose of this
work is to arrange synthetically, in its wide connection
with the mechanics of the Unconscious thus founded, the
whole psychical development of man as shown from the
analytically recognized importance of the birth trauma and
in the continually recurring attempts to overcome it. We
notice, moreover, with astonishment how, without compulsion, we succeed in linking the deepest biological layer of the
Unconscious to the highest manifest content of the mental
productions of mankind. In this way the foundation and
the principle correspond with, and harmoniously supplement
one another, or as Freud himself expresses it in his latest
work: " What has belonged to the depths in the individual
psychical life, becomes the highest in the human psyche in
the sense of our valuation, through the formation of an
ideal."[1]

Whilst attempting in the following pages to trace the
mechanism of this " ideal-formation " in the development
of man right to its biological basis, we recognize through
all the complicated transformations of the Unconscious—
which Psychoanalysis first taught us to understand—how
the deepest biological content ultimately almost unchanged,
though indiscernible only through our own inner repression,
yet remains tangible as manifest form even in the highest

[1] *The Ego and the Id,* 1923.

intellectual accomplishments.   There is apparent in this a
normal and universally valid psycho-biological law, the full
significance of which is neither to be estimated nor exhausted
within the compass of the arguments we have outlined here.
But the chief purpose of this work is to draw attention to this
biologically based law of the form which determines the content,
and here and there to suggest to the imagination rather
than to wish to solve, the wider problems which loom up from
behind.   But to be able to set forth the whole problem at all,
and to risk at least the first steps towards its solution, this
we owe to the instrument of investigation and to the way of
thinking which Freud has given us in Psychoanalysis.

THE TRAUMA OF BIRTH

THE ANALYTIC SITUATION

As a preliminary to my task of pursuing a little further the investigation of the Unconscious from my psychoanalytic experiences and observations, I should like to refer to a fundamental principle which has hitherto guided psycho-analytic investigation. Freud has occasionally remarked that Psychoanalysis was really invented by the first patient whom Breuer treated in the year 1881, and whose case (Anna O——) was published many years later (1895) in the *Studien über Hysterie*. The young girl, who understood only English in her nervous states, called the soothing hypnotic speeches to her doctor the *talking cure*, or jokingly referred to them as *chimney sweeping*. And in later years, when hostility was shown to psychoanalytic experiences and results on account of their astonishing novelty, and they were criticized as being productions of the author's perverted imagination, Freud used to hold up against these stupid objections the argument that no human brain would have been able to invent such facts and connections, if they had not been persistently forced on it by a series of similar observations. In this sense, therefore, one may say that not only the basic idea of Psychoanalysis but also its further development is largely due to the patients whose valuable efforts supplied an accumulation of material which, though fragmentary in character and unequal in worth, was eventually condensed by means of Freud's power of observation into general notions, principles, and laws.

Only in this path of investigation, along which Psychoanalysis has gone step by step, striving against all kinds of resistances, can Freud's statement, that the patient somehow is really always right although he himself does not know how and why, be fully estimated.   But the analyst has to show him this by revealing connections which were repressed, by filling in memories previously forgotten, and by disclosing the " meaning " of the illness and of its symptoms.   Psychologically too the patient is right, because the Unconscious—although by means of pathologic distortion—speaks through him as it has spoken formerly through the mouths of geniuses, prophets, founders of religions, artists, philosophers, and discoverers.   For not only is the psychological knowledge which is based on intuition a step towards the grasping and understanding of the Unconscious, but the capability of recognition itself presupposes to a certain extent a removal and overcoming of repression, behind which we can " reveal " the things sought for.   The scientific value of psychoanalyses applied to others lies in the fact that they enable us, often by great effort, to remove the repressions in others which we cannot detect in ourselves; and thus we gain insight into new fields of the Unconscious.   If I now refer to the objective method of investigation by Psychoanalysis, it is because, under the abundance of astonishing impressions of the same kind, I was forced to the conclusion that the Unconscious is once more right at the very point where hitherto we dared to follow it only hesitatingly and incredulously.

In a number of analyses, most of which were successfully

accomplished, I noticed that in the end-phase of the analysis the *healing process* was *quite regularly* represented by the Unconscious in the typical *birth symbolism*, which to a large extent is already known to us. I have also attempted, in a hitherto unpublished work (written in the winter of 1921-22), entitled *Zum Verständnis der Libidoentwicklung im Heilungsvorgang* ("Concerning the Understanding of the Libido Development in the Healing Process "),[1] to show the theoretical importance of these astonishing facts in connection with other characteristic features of the healing process (for instance, the identification with the analyst, etc.). I mentioned there that it is obviously a matter of the well-known *rebirth-phantasy*, in which the patient's desire for recovery expresses its accomplishment. In the same way patients frequently speak, in their convalescence, of feeling " new born." I emphasize also the unmistakable part of the work of sublimation, which lies in the fact that the patient is now able to renounce the infantile libido fixation, expressed in the Œdipus complex, in favour of the analysis. He does this finally by renouncing the phantasy of the infant child, which he—as the mother—wishes to present to the father, and by considering himself the new-born (spiritual) child (of the analyst).

In spite of this conception, regularly emerging from the analytic material which I there briefly mentioned, and which without doubt seems justified within the limits of the healing process, I was struck on the one hand by the infantile character of the " rebirth-phantasy," and on the other hand by its " anagogic " character, which has been valued to excess by Jung to the neglect of its libidinal tendencies, and hence has been misleading theoretically.

[1] See *Internat. Zschr. für Psychoanalyse*, ix., 4, 1923.

The existence of such ideas has never been denied;[1] what puzzled me was that the real basis of thoughts of this kind was missing.

So I left the matter, till one day, in a specially obvious case, it became clear to me that the strongest resistance to the severance of the libido transference at the end of the analysis is expressed in the form of the earliest infantile *fixation on the mother*. In numerous dreams belonging to this end-phase the finally undeniable fact forced itself upon us again and again that the fixation on the mother, which seems to be at the bottom of the analytic fixation (transference), includes the earliest physiological relation to the mother's womb. This rendered the regularity of the rebirth-phantasy intelligible and its underlying reality analytically comprehensible. The patient's " rebirth-phantasy " is simply a repetition in the analysis of his own birth. The freeing of the libido from its object, the analyst, seems to correspond to an *exact reproduction* of the first separation from the first libido object, namely of the new-born child from the mother.

Since patients, irrespective of sex, and uninfluenced by the analyst (who was himself ignorant of the fact), seemed to create this terminal situation quite regularly, it became clear that this was a matter of fundamental import, and that here again one would have to have the courage to follow on the track of the Unconscious and to take it seriously. It is proved, then, without doubt that the essential part of the work of analysis, the solving and freeing of the libido " neurotically " fixed on the analyst, is really neither

---

[1] *Cf.* Freud, " History of an Infantile Neurosis," *Collected Papers*, vol. iii., p. 583 ff., and the discussion involved there which we continue and attempt to solve in the last chapter but one.

more nor less than allowing the patient to repeat with better success in the analysis the separation from the mother. But this is by no means to be taken metaphorically in any way—not even in the psychological sense. For in the analytic situation the patient repeats, biologically, as it were, the period of pregnancy, and at the conclusion of the analysis—*i.e.*, the re-separation from the substitute object —he repeats his own birth for the most part quite faithfully in all its details. *The analysis finally turns out to be a belated accomplishment of the incompleted mastery of the birth trauma.*

This conclusion, to which I was forced by a mass of heterogeneous material, but especially by dreams which will be published in a wider connection, immediately aroused in me certain objections to which I will only allude, since they were soon removed by further experiences. It is possible, I reflected, that owing to my individuality, or owing to a special application of the technique which, according to the classical Freudian method, begins, though it certainly does not end, with the disintegration of " complexes "—it is possible, however, that I may be driving back the Ego of the patient to earlier and yet earlier libido positions,[1] so that finally it would not be surprising if, in the terminal stage of the analysis, the last flight of the libido were to the intrauterine stage. One might even hold that this would be the final result in the case of very prolonged analyses. On the other hand, I would like to emphasize that first of all it is not a matter of a mere phenomenon of regression, in the meaning of the "womb-phantasy" familiar to us all, which has long been considered by

[1] Ferenczi accepted a similar assumption for the process of disintegration in progressive paralysis. Hollos-Ferenczi, *Psychoanalysis and the Psychic Disorders of General Paresis.*

Psychoanalysis to be a typical primal phantasy. But it is a matter of much more substantial reproductions under the influence of a real repetition compulsion. Further, my analyses, as far as I know, are some of the shortest in duration, lasting from four to eight months at the very longest.

But this and other thoughts of a similar kind, which came to me at the beginning, soon disappeared under the following overwhelming impression. In focussing attention analytically on these facts one noticed that people, theoretically and therapeutically entirely uninfluenced, showed from the very beginning of their treatment the same tendency to identify the analytic situation with the intrauterine state. In some cases, started at the same time, but differing completely in type and character of neurosis, the patients of both sexes identified the analyst with the mother from the beginning in a very decided manner, and in their dreams and reactions they put themselves back again into the position of the unborn.[1] Hence the real transference-libido, which we have to solve analytically in both sexes, is the mother-libido, as it existed in the pre-natal physiological connection between mother and child.

When one has become more accustomed to this conception it almost seems as if one had always tacitly, or rather unconsciously, worked with it in view; but at the same time one notices with astonishment how much goes to support it, how many dark and enigmatic problems in analysis, and especially in the healing process, vanish at a stroke as soon

---

[1] I shall also publish the proof for this just as it came under my observation, in a work *On the Technique of Dream Interpretation in Psychoanalyses* (already partly published in the first volume of *The Technique of Psychoanalysis*).

as one is able to grasp the full meaning and the fundamental importance of this fact.

Above all, the analytic situation, which historically has developed from the hypnotic state,[1] seems to challenge a direct comparison between the Unconscious and the primal state. Consider only the restful position in a half-darkened room, the dreamy state of phantasy (hallucinations) almost free from any of the claims of reality, the presence and at the same time the uncertainty of the libido object, and so on. This unconscious conception of the analytic situation explains why the patient, in his associations, which unconsciously have ultimately in view the primal mother situation, is able spontaneously to go back into his childhood and so bring the analyst to recognize the importance of infantile material and infantile impressions. Also the consciously directed associations correspond to an asymptotic approach to that primary attitude of transference in which the patient unconsciously puts himself from the beginning.

The increased memory capacity, especially for forgotten (repressed) impressions of childhood, occurring in the analysis, is thus to be explained (like the similar phenomenon in hypnosis) by the tendency of the Unconscious, encouraged by the suggestion of the doctor (transference), to reproduce the real, that is, the primal, situation, as automatically happens, for example, in the likewise hypermnesic state of the dream, of certain neurotic conditions (*double conscience*)

[1] The hypnotic sleep, as all similar conditions in the dreams of rebirth, appears as a typical element of the intrauterine state; it may be assumed that the essence of hypnosis itself, the capacity of being hypnotized, goes back to the primal relation of the child to the mother. Moreover, Paul Bjerre expressed a similar thought many years ago (*Das Wesen der Hypnose*).

or of psychotic regressive formations (the so-called " archaic thoughts "). In this sense all memories of infancy must, to a certain extent, be considered as " cover-memories "; and the whole capacity for reproduction in general would be due to the fact that the " primal scene " can never be remembered, because the most painful of all " memories," namely the birth trauma, is linked to it by " association." The almost incredible findings of the technique of " free associations " received in this way their biological basis. But we will not yield to the temptation to tackle the whole psycho-physical problem of memory from this Archimedean point, from which the whole process of repression starts, and which is analytically easy to undo.[1] One can only advance the supposition that the primal repression of the birth trauma may be considered as the cause of memory in general—that is, of the partial capacity for remembering. Thus the fact that detached memories remain with one as if specially chosen out shows on the one hand that they have been absorbed by the primal repression, and on the other hand that they will be reproduced[2] later on as a substitute for the really repressed, the primal trauma.

It is therefore quite natural that the analytic resistance to the giving up of this phase of the mother-binding, once

[1] See the last chapter.

[2] It would lead us too far to pursue this important theme in detail. In the case of one patient with a phenomenal memory, it was analytically easy to establish that her entire skill rested on the intense repression of a severe birth trauma. Her whole association mechanism was built up on numerous dates of birth, taken from relatives, acquaintances, and historical persons. From this a new light fell on the problematical analysis of the occurrence of numbers, in which almost always birth dates appear as the centres of association. See also further remarks below as to time.

really experienced, should concern the father (substitute), who actually initiated the primal severance from the mother and so became the first and lasting enemy. The task, then, of the analyst, who in the course of the treatment represents both objects of the infantile libido, is to sever this primal fixation on the mother, a task which the patient was unable to accomplish alone. The analyst has also to deal with the libido thus freed and to make it capable of being further transferred to the father or mother image, according to the sex of the patient. When the analyst succeeds in overcoming the primal resistance, namely the mother-fixation, with regard to his own person in the transference relation, then a definite term is fixed for the analysis, within which period the patient repeats automatically the new severance from the mother (substitute) figure, in the form of the reproduction of his own birth. Thus the frequent question as to when an analysis is at an end seems in this sense to be answered. A definite length of time for the termination of this process (*i.e.*, birth) is naturally necessary and maintains its biological explanation and justification from the following conception— viz., that the analysis has to make it possible for the patient subsequently to overcome the birth trauma by fixing a corresponding time-limit, which from this therapeutic standpoint can, to a great extent, be regulated.[1] Naturally the patient constantly shows the tendency behind all his resistances to prolong[2] indefinitely the analytic situation

[1] *Cf.* my explanation in the joint work with Ferenczi, *Development of Psychoanalysis*.

[2] It is well known how frequently the length of pregnancy (seven to ten months) is preferred, but this concerns not merely the familiar phantasy of pregnancy (child by father), but in the deepest layer refers to one's own birth.

Cf. also the well-known cures of Déjèrine, who treats his patients

which yields him such considerable satisfaction. And from the very beginning this tendency must become the object of analysis.

This also follows quite automatically through a strict observance of the Freudian rule, which prescribes that the patient must be seen daily at the same time and for a full hour. Each of these hours represents for the patient's Unconscious an analysis in miniature with the renewed fixation and gradual solving, which, as is well known,[1] the patients often dislike very much at the beginning. They already take the daily dismissal in the meaning of the freeing from the mother as a too active therapy, whilst on the other hand the general inclination to run away from the analyst is to be explained as the tendency towards an all too direct repetition of the birth trauma, which is just what the analysis has to replace by a gradual detachment.

---

as prisoners; locks them up in a dark room from everyone, and has their food brought to them through an opening; after a certain time they are glad to be discharged from this dungeon.

[1] Many of them cannot wait till the analyst sends them away, but wish to decide this themselves, and often look at the time; others —or even the same—want to shake hands at their departure, etc. *Cf.* the passing symptom described by Ferenczi, " Schwindelemp-findung am Schluss der Analysenstunde " (*Zschr.*, 1914) (" Sensation of Dizziness at the end of the Hour of Analysis "), where the patient reacts to the psychical trauma of sudden separation with an analogous disturbance of his equilibrium, as an hysterical symptom.

INFANTILE ANXIETY

THE immediate conclusion which can be deduced from these analytic experiences and from the significance they have for us is that the patient's Unconscious uses the analytic healing process in order to repeat the trauma of birth and thus partially to abreact it. But before we can understand how the birth trauma can be expressed in such various neurotic symptoms, we must first trace its general human effect in the development of the normal individual, particularly in childhood. We shall take as our guiding principle Freud's statement that all anxiety goes back originally to the anxiety at birth (dyspnœa).

If we look at the psychical development of the child from this point of view, it may be said that the human being needs many years—namely, his whole childhood—in which to overcome this first intensive trauma in an approximately normal way. Every child has anxiety, and from the standpoint of the average healthy adult, one can, with a certain amount of justification, designate the childhood of individuals as their normal neurosis. Only this may continue into adult life in the case of certain individuals, the neurotics, who therefore remain infantile or are called infantile.

Instead of numerous examples with the same simple mechanism, let us investigate the typical case of infantile anxiety which occurs when the child is left alone *in a dark room* (usually the bedroom at bed-time). This situation reminds the child, who still is close to the experience of the primal trauma, of the womb situation—with the important difference that the child is now consciously separated from the mother, whose womb is only " symbolically " replaced by the dark room or warm bed. The anxiety disappears, according to Freud's brilliant observation, as soon as the child again becomes conscious of the existence (the nearness) of the loved person (contact, voice, etc).[1]

From this example we can understand the anxiety mechanism, which is repeated almost unaltered in cases of phobia (claustrophobia, fear of railways, tunnels, travelling, etc.), as the unconscious reproduction of the anxiety at birth. And at the same time we can study the elements of symbol formation, and last but not least, the importance of the fact of being separated from the mother, and the calming " therapeutic " effect of the reunion with her, although only a partial or " symbolic " one.

Whilst reserving for later chapters more detailed discussion about these prospects which promise so much, let us look at a second situation, likewise typical of childish anxiety, which is nearer to the actual deeply repressed facts. We mean the universal childish *fear of animals*. We must not look for its explanation in an inherited human instinct of fear, in spite of its frequent relation to beasts of prey (carnivorous animals such as the wolf). For it is obvious that such a fear, could not relate to the domesticated animals, used thousands of years ago, whose harmlessness was experienced and met with by numerous generations of adults, in the same way as was the danger from beasts of prey. One would need to go further back to the primeval times of man—or even to his first biological stage (as do Stanley Hall and others) —and thence to the wild ancestors of our domesticated animals, in order to explain a typical anxiety reaction,

---

[1] See *Three Contributions to the Theory of Sex*, 1918, p. 84, footnote.

which has its origin in our individual development. There are other, namely psychological (symbolic), factors, which are decisive for the choice of these objects of fear, which occurs originally according to the size of the animal (horse, cow, etc.), impressing the child. As the analysis of childish phobias has clearly shown, the size or fatness (circumference of the body) of the animals causing fear refers to the state of pregnancy of which the child, as we can show, has more than a vague memory. The beasts of prey, then, provide a rationalization, also sufficient, apparently, for grown-up psychologists, of the wish—through the desire to be eaten—to get back again into the mother's animal womb. The significance of animals as a father substitute, which in the psychology of neuroses Freud has emphasized for the understanding of Totemism, remains not only undisturbed by this conception, but maintains a deepened biological significance, showing how, through the displacement of anxiety on to the father, the renunciation of the mother, necessary for the sake of life, is assured. For this feared father prevents the return to the mother and thereby the releasing of the much more painful primal anxiety, which is related to the mother's genitals as the place of birth, and later transferred to objects taking the place of the genitals.

The equally frequent anxiety about small animals, which, however, is usually accompanied by dread, has the same foundation, and the " uncanniness " of these objects clearly betrays this origin. From the analysis of such phobias or anxiety dreams, which have been found even in men, although less frequently than in women, it is clearly proved that the feeling of weirdness or uncanniness in the presence of these small creeping animals, such as mice, snakes, frogs, beetles, etc., can be traced to their peculiar ability completely to disappear into small holes in the earth. They therefore exhibit the wish to return into the maternal hiding-place as completely accomplished. And the feeling of dread which clings to them arises because they materialize one's own tendency, namely, to go back into mother, and one is afraid because they might creep into one's own body.[1] Whilst one is able to go into *large* animals, still in the meaning of the primal situation, although repressed (anxiety), the dread of *small* animals lies in the danger that they can enter one's own body. Moreover, all such small animals as insects, etc., were long ago recognized by Psycho-analysis as symbolic representations of children or embryos, not only on account of their small size, but also because of the possibility of their growing bigger (symbol of fertility).[2]

[1] A little girl of three years, who feared small dogs just as much as if not more than large ones, was also afraid of insects (flies, bees, etc.). When asked by her mother why she was afraid of these small animals, which could not harm her, the little one replied without any hesitation, " Yet they can swallow me !" But at the approach of small dogs, she makes the same characteristic movements of defence that a grown-up person makes with a mouse; she bends her knees so low, at the same time pressing her legs close together, that her little dress touches the ground, and she can cover herself as if she wanted to prevent them from " creeping in." Another time, when directly asked by her mother as to the cause of her fear of bees, she explained with many contradictions that she wanted to go into the bee's body and yet again not to go in.

[2] Recently in Freud's *History of an Infantile Neurosis*, p. 569, *Collected Papers*, vol. iii., he shows that in the fear of butterflies the opening and the shutting of the wings is the disturbing factor, which again clearly reminds one of the opening in the body (*cf.* the widespread mythical motive of symplegades, or closing rocks). The spider is a clear symbol of the dreaded mother in whose net one is caught. *Cf.* the " unconscious birth phantasy " which Ferenczi quotes from the description in a diary of a patient's attack of anxiety (" Introjection and Transference," p. 70 in *Contributions to Psychoanalysis*): " Hypochondria surrounds my soul like

But they become a penis symbol or rather a penis ideal just because of their capacity *completely* to go in and disappear into holes, etc., whereby their essential peculiarity, the special smallness, which has led to their being interpreted even as spermatozoa or ova, directly indicates the womb as their place of abode. Thus the (large) animal represents at first the pleasure-laden, then the anxiety-laden, mother symbol. Later, by displacement of the anxiety into a phobia, the animal becomes an inhibiting father substitute. Finally, by means of observation of the sexuality of animals and of small animals, which symbolize the fœtus as well as the penis, it again becomes invested with maternal libido.

This explains why a number of small animals became *soul-animals* in popular beliefs. The best-known example is that of the snake, whose phallic significance can undoubtedly be traced back to the ease with which it can completely enter and disappear into a hole (in the earth).[1]

This is shown in the well-known belief in animal-spirits of the Australians and certain Central Asiatic tribes. According to this belief, children go into the mother, mostly through

---

a fine mist, or rather like a cobweb, just as a fungus covers the swamp. I have the feeling as though I were sticking in a bog, as though I had to stretch out my head so as to be able to breathe. I want to tear the cobweb, to tear it. But no, I can't do it ! The web is fastened somewhere—the props would have to be pulled out on which it hangs. If that can't be done, one would have slowly to work one's way through the net in order to get air. Man surely is not here to be veiled in such a cobweb, suffocated, and robbed of the light of the sun.''

[1] That the peculiarity, especially in large snakes, of swallowing their prey alive and whole, thus causing their body to swell up, belongs to this circle of ideas, appears to me just as certain as in the case of the other remarkable fact of their shedding their skin (rebirth).

the navel, in the form of little animals. Thus the natives of Cape Bedford believe "that boys go into the mother's womb in the form of a snake, and girls in the form of snipe."[1] The quite primitive identity of child and phallus —the phallus goes completely into the woman and there grows into a child—appears later in popular beliefs and in fairy tales, as a soul endowed with a body, where the soul of a sleeping or dead person creeps out of the mouth in the form of such animals as mouse, snake, etc. Then after a while it enters again through the mouth into the same human being (dream) or into another one (fertilization, new birth).[2] Here may be added the very ancient popular practice of picturing the womb as an animal. This belief hitherto has found no explanation,[3] but presumably is also connected with the idea of the animal which has crept into the womb and has not come out again, and thus finally refers to the *content* of the impregnated uterus. In Braunschweig it is the custom not to let the child during the first twenty-four

[1] See F. Reitzenstein's article " Aberglaube " in *Handworterbuch der Sexualwissenschaft*, edited by Max Marcuse, 1923, p. 5.

[2] In the Malay Fanany-fairy tale, the East African snake of death develops into a soul-worm, which appears from the grave, after about six or eight months, by means of a bamboo reed stuck in the earth (according to H. L. Held, *Schlangenkultus Atlas Africanus*, vol. iii. München, 1922).

[3] That this animal is most frequently a toad, which creeps (*verkriechen, kröte*) into dark and inaccessible holes, would seem to agree with this idea. See " Die Kröte, ein Bild der Gebärmutter," by Karl Spiess (*Mitra*, i., column 209 ff., 1914, No. 8). Even in ancient Egypt the goddess of birth was thought of as frog-headed (see Jacoby and Spiegelberg, " Der Frosch als Symbol der Auferstehung bei den Ägyptern," *Sphinx*, vii.); on the other hand, the head of the " uterus-toad " shows at times human characteristics (see picture in Spiess, *l.c.*, column 217). *Cf.* Ernest Fuhrmann on the same significance of the toad in ancient Mexico: *Mexiko*, iii., p. 20 ff. (*Kulturen der Erde*, vol. xiii. Darmstadt, 1922).

hours after its birth lie by the mother's side, " otherwise the uterus can find no rest and scratches about in the woman's body, like a large mouse."[1] " It can also creep forth during sleep through the mouth, bathe, and return in the same way," as in the legend recorded by Panzer of a woman pilgrim who lay in the grass for rest (*Beitr. z. d. Mythologie*, ii., 195). If it cannot find the way back the woman becomes sterile.

The reference to these typical childish situations of anxiety and their parallels in folklore should suffice to show what we mean. In thoroughly investigating the conditions under which the child's anxiety arises, we find that the anxiety experienced at parturition really continues, undisposed of, to influence the child. And every opportunity, which somehow " reminds " the child—mostly in a " symbolic " way—of the birth trauma is used again and again for the abreaction of the undisposed-of affect (*cf.* for instance the frequency of *pavor nocturnus* in children). If one ventures to accept literally and seriously the origin of the anxiety-affect which Freud recognized as arising in the process of birth—and one is forced to do so by a number of experiences—then it is easy to realize *how every infantile utterance of anxiety or fear is really a partial disposal of the birth anxiety.*

We will approach later, in the discussion of the pleasure-pain-mechanism, the pressing question as to how the tendency to repeat so strong an affect of pain arises. But we wish to dwell for the moment on the equally indubitable analytic fact that, just as the anxiety at birth forms the basis of every anxiety or fear, so *every pleasure has as its final aim the re-establishment of the intrauterine primal pleasure.*

[1] See article " Aberglaube," *l.c.*

2

The child's normal functions, the assimilation of nourishment (sucking) and the expulsion of the product assimilated, both of which functions analysis recognizes as libidinal, betray the tendency to continue as long as possible the unlimited freedom of the pre-natal state. As we know from the analyses of neurotics, the Unconscious never gives up this claim, which the Ego has to set aside in favour of social adjustment, and the Unconscious, in its predominating states, which approach the primal condition (dream, neurosis, coma), is ready every time to come forward with this regressive tendency.

More clearly still do the " childish faults," resulting from a too persistent clinging to these sources of pleasure, show the origin and tendency of this libido-gratification. I mean such "faults " as sucking on the one hand, and wetting and dirtying themselves on the other, when these go beyond a certain length of time or to a certain degree of intensity (for instance, in the exquisite " neurotic" symptom of enuresis nocturna). In the consciously uncontrollable and apparently automatic ejection of urine and discharge of fæces ("as proof of love " for the mother) the child behaves as if it were still in the womb; *inter fæces et urinas*.[1] The proverbial connection between fear and defecation rests on a similar mechanism. The temporary (or, after weaning, the complete) substitution of a finger for the mother's breast shows on the other hand the child's first attempt to replace the mother's body by its own ("identification "), or by a part of its own. And the enigmatic preference for the toes clearly betrays the tendency to re-establish the

[1] The water closet appears in dreams as a typical representation for the womb (Steckel, *Die Sprache des Traumes*, 1911).

intrauterine position of the body.[1] From sucking as well as from the pleasurable discharge of the urine (enuresis), the way discovered by Psychoanalysis leads to the " childish fault " *par excellence*, masturbation of the genitals (*cf.* also the later replacing of enuresis by pollution). This leads to and helps to prepare for the final and sublimest substitution for the reunion with the mother, namely, the sexual act. The attempt to associate with sexuality the mother's genitals, originally invested with anxiety, causes the guilt feeling, because the mother anxiety became attached to the father according to the mechanism of the phobia. In this way the partial change of the primal anxiety into the (sexual) guilt feeling occurs. One can observe clearly how the fear of animals originally referring to the mother changes into fear of the father, resting on sexual repression. Then it can become perfectly rationalized through displacement to robbers, criminals, black men, etc., according to the phobia mechanism. Here the so-called real fear arising from danger comes into existence as a connecting link and as an outlet for the displaced primal anxiety. Thus the change of the claustrophobia referring to the mother into the anxiety of something entering onself referring to the father completely corresponds to the (child's) attitude to the large (motherly) and to the small (phallic) animals.

At this point we anticipate from the psychoanalytic side an objection which we hope easily to dispose of. The general

[1] According to a verbal communication, the Viennese child specialist, J. K. Friedjung, was able on many occasions to observe children who came into the world with a finger in the mouth. This shows the tendency to an immediate substitution of the mother in *statu nascendi*. Recent experiments on the reflex excitability of the foetus have been able to show that already in the sixth or seventh month sucking reflexes can be produced.

validity of the experience that the child's every anxiety consists of the anxiety at birth (and the child's every pleasure aims at the re-establishing of the intrauterine primal pleasure) could be called in question in view of the so-called *castration anxiety*, which has recently been so strongly emphasized.   Yet it seems to me quite intelligible that the childish primal anxiety, in the course of its development, should cling more especially to the genitals just on account of their vaguely imagined (or remembered) actual biological relation to birth (and procreation).   It is conceivable, indeed obvious, that precisely the female genitals, being the place of the birth trauma, should soon again become the chief object of the anxiety-affect originally arising there.   Thus the importance of the castration fear is based, as Stärcke thinks,[1] on the primal castration at birth, that is, on the separation of the child from the mother.[2]

But it does not seem quite appropriate to speak of " castration " where, as yet, there is no clearer relation of anxiety to the genitals, than is given by the fact of birth from the (female) genitals.[3]   This conception finds a strong heuristic support in that it solves the riddle of the ubiquity of the " castration complex " in a natural way by deriving it from the indisputable universality of the act of birth.   This is a point of view which proves to be of the greatest importance for the complete understanding and also for the real foundation of other primal phantasies.   We believe that we are

---

[1] A. Stärcke, " Psychoanalysis and Psychiatry " (*The Internat. Journal of Ps.A.*, vol. ii., 1921.

[2] In dreams at the end of the analytic cure I found the phallus often used as " symbol " of the umbilical cord.

[3] See also Freud, " The Infantile Genital Organization of the Libido," *Collected Papers*, vol. ii. (quoted only after the conclusion of this work)

now better able to understand why the castration threat should cause such a stupendous and lasting effect on the child—and, moreover, why childish anxiety and the guilt feeling brought on by birth and arising from it cannot be avoided by any kind of educational measure or removed by the usual analytic explanations.[1] The threat of castration hits not only the vaguely remembered primal trauma and the undisposed-of anxiety representing it, but also a second trauma, consciously experienced and painful in character, though later obliterated by repression, namely weaning, the intensity and persistence of which falls far short of that of the first trauma, but owes a great part of its " traumatic " effect to it. Only in the third place, then, does there appear the genital trauma of castration *regularly phantasied* in the history of the individual and, at most, experienced as a threat.[2] But this, just on account of its unreality, seems predisposed to take upon itself the greatest part of the natal anxiety-affect as guilt feeling, which, as in the meaning of the biblical fall of man, actually proves to be connected with the differentiation of the sexes, the difference in the sexual organs and the sexual functions. The deepest Unconscious which always remains sexually

[1] See in addition Melanie Klein, " The Development of a Child," *Internat. Journal of Ps.A.*, vol. iv., 1923.

[2] The typical duality, which as symbol of defence and consolation for castration should compensate the loss of one irreplaceable member (often by a multiplicity), seems originally to belong to the weaning trauma, and to go back to the possibility of obtaining nourishment at both breasts, whereby actually the one breast replaces the " loss " of the other. Also the " symbolic " use of the testicles proves to be not infrequently a point of transition between the breasts and the penis, like the udder of a cow (*cf.* Stekel's symbolic equation of " pairs of organs "). On another level, the duality of the castration defence seems to serve infantile irony in face of the lies of the grown-ups (see also *infra*, pp. 21-2).

indifferent (bi-sexual) knows nothing of this and knows only the first primal anxiety of the universal human act of birth.

In comparison with the painfully experienced actual traumata of birth and weaning, a real threat of castration seems even to make easier the normal discharge of the primal anxiety as genital guilt feeling, in so far and just as soon as the child has discovered the insincerity of the castration threat as of all other untruths of adults. In contrast to the primal trauma, then, the castration phantasy, which is soon unmasked as an empty threat, can occur rather as a consolation since the severance cannot take place.[1] From this point we are led directly to the infantile sexual theories (see later, p. 32 f.) which refuse to recognize " castration " (the female genitals), obviously so as to be able to deny along with it the trauma of birth (primal-separation).

It should be noticed, moreover, that every playful use of the tragic primal motive, which occurs with the consciousness of unreality, works in a pleasurable way in that it advantageously denies the reality of any trauma. Examples of this are the typical children's *games* from the earliest "hiding" (hide-and-seek) to the games of swinging, trains, dolls, and doctor,[2] which, moreover, as Freud very soon recognized, contain the same elements as the corresponding neurotic symptoms, only with positive pleasurable signs. The game of hiding (also conjuring), which children tirelessly repeat, represents the situation of separation

[1] The same mechanism of solace or consolation is again to be found in the faulty acts of losing things, recognized as actions of sacrifice. One cuts oneself off from a valuable part of one's ego instead of being completely " cut off " (" the ring of Polycrates," which is thrown into the sea, but which comes to light again in the fish's belly).

[2] The last two with direct reference to childbirth (doll = fœtus in dream).

(and of finding again) as not of a serious kind; the rhythmic games of movement (swinging, hopping, etc.) simply repeat the rhythm felt in the embryonic state. This rhythm shows, in the neurotic symptom of dizziness, the other side of the Janus head. Soon the child's every game will somehow be subordinated to the viewpoint of its unreality. And Psychoanalysis has been able to show how, from the child's game, the higher and the highest pleasure-giving unrealities, namely, phantasy and art, emerge.[1] Even in the highest forms of these pretended realities, as, for example, in the Greek tragedies, we are in a position to *enjoy anxiety* and *horror* because we abreact these primal affects, in the meaning of Aristotle's catharsis, just as the child now works off the separation from the mother, originally full of dread, in its game of willing concealment,[2] which can easily and often be broken off and repeated at the child's pleasure.

The child's constant proneness to anxiety, which originates in the birth trauma and is transferable to almost anything, is expressed in a more direct, and so to speak, a more biological way in the child's characteristic attitude towards death, important also from a general point of view. What astonished us at first was not the fact that the child knows nothing at all of the idea of death, but that here also, as in the sexual realm, it is, for a long time, not in a position to accept the facts and explanations as to its real significance. It is one of Freud's greatest merits that he has called our attention to the child's negative idea of death, which is expressed, for example, in the fact that it treats a dead

[1] Freud, *Der Dichter und das Phantasieren*, 1908.
[2] In fairy tales also, as, for example, in the Seven Kids, the concealment has the significance of birth and rescue, that is, return to the mother's womb in the case of external danger.

person as one temporarily absent. It is well known, also, that the Unconscious never gives up this idea, to which not only the ever-reviving belief in immortality bears witness but also the fact that we dream of the dead as living.

It would be quite wrong, too, to suppose, according to our intellectualist attitude, that the child cannot accept the idea of death on account of its painfulness and its unpleasant character; this is not the case for the reason that the child turns away from the idea of it *a priori*, without having any understanding of its content. In general the child cannot be said to have any abstract idea of death, and reacts only to cases that have been actually experienced or to those that have been described (explained) to it in connection with the persons well known to it. To be dead has the same meaning for the child as to be away (Freud) —that is, to be *separated*—and this directly touches on the primal trauma. The child thus accepts the conscious idea of death by unconsciously identifying it with the primal trauma. It may, therefore, seem brutal to adults that the child should want the death of an unwished-for rival, a new little brother or sister whose intrusion is not pleasing to it: this is much the same as when we ourselves say to someone, he can go to the devil—that is, leave us alone. Only the child betrays a far better knowledge than the adult of the original meaning of this ''manner of speech,'' when, for example, it advises the intruding little brother or sister to go back to where he came from. The child means this quite seriously and can do so again on the strength of those dim memories of the place whence children come. And so with the thought of death is connected from the beginning a strong unconscious sense of pleasure associated with the return to the mother's womb. This pleasurable affect has been maintained undiminished through the whole history of mankind, from the primitive customs of cremation to the spiritual return in the form of an astral body.

But it is not merely the human *idea* of death that has this libidinal background, for man also unconsciously plays the trump-card of prenatal existence—the only condition of which we have any experience apart from our conscious life— against the idea of destruction in death, consciously recognized as real. When the child wants to remove a competitor disturbing to his peace, and therefore wishes he were dead, he can do this only by means of his own pleasurable memory of the place he came from and whence the little brother or sister also came—from the mother. One could also say that he wishes himself back again in the place where there is no kind of disturbance from outside. In the childish wish for the death of others, the justification for emphasizing their own unconscious wish element is made clear from the understanding of the self-reproaches with which neurotics regularly react at the accidental realization of such a wish. When one loses a closely connected person of either sex, this loss reminds one again of the primal separation from the mother; and the painful task of disengaging the libido from this person (recognized by Freud in the process of *mourning*) corresponds to a psychical repetition of the primal trauma. In the different human customs of mourning it is undoubtedly clear, as recently shown by Reik in a lecture,[1] that the mourner tries to identify himself with the dead, showing how he envies him the return to the mother. The marked impressions, which the premature death of a brother or sister leaves in the Unconscious of the survivors, who

---

[1] "Tabnit, König von Sidon " (Wiener Psychoanalytic Association, March, 1923).

later often become neurotic, clearly show the strange after-
effects of this identification with the dead.   This not seldom
expresses itself in the fact that the person in question spends
his life, as it were, in perpetual mourning, that is, in a state
which is adapted in a bewildering way to the dead person's
supposed place of abode.   Many neuroses, taken as a whole,
can be understood as such an embryonal continuance of the
prematurely cut-off existence of a brother or sister.   And
melancholy frequently shows the same mechanism as a reaction to an actual death.[1]

As one clearly sees in analyses, the child envies the dead
the happiness of return to the mother and so links his real
jealousy to the new brother or sister, generally at the period
of pregnancy, that is, at the time of the abode in the mother.
The well-known adjustment to the fact of the new competitor, on the other hand, begins soon after its birth (the
child as a living doll) by identification with the mother (the
child from the father).   In the child's unconscious tendency
to identify itself in the mother's womb with the child
whose imminent arrival has been sufficiently announced
lies the decisive factor, which in the meaning of psychoanalytic investigations might be described as the *Trauma
of the Second Child* (brother or sister trauma).   Its essential
factor consists in the fact that the later coming child
materializes the deepest wish tendency of the already
present child to be again in the mother, and, as it were,
spoils once for all the chances of ever returning there.
This can become a determining factor for the whole further
attitude and development of the first or previously born

[1] It would be worth while in the anamneses of melancholics to
find out whether they had experienced a death in the family in their
childhood.

(see *The Psychology of the Youngest*, p. 107, " Heroic Compensation "). From this many otherwise unintelligible traits in adult love life (neurotic limitation of children, etc.), as also certain neurotic organic sufferings of women, become analytically accessible (pseudo-sterility, etc.).

The identification of death with the return to the mother also explains why the dead must not be disturbed in their rest and why such a disturbance is regarded as the greatest punishment.   This proves the secondary nature of the whole rebirth phantasy, which has no other meaning than to re-establish the original condition and remain there.   This is shown also by various biological facts which lead to the exclusion of the ethical-anagogic element of the rebirth idea, held erroneously by Jung to be essential.[1]   A certain species of *Cichlides* (mouth-brooders) forms a particularly instructive example.   The female carries the spawn till their maturity in a pouch in her throat.[2]   In the existing North African species, *Haplochromis strigigena*, which fasten their eggs to plants and stones, the mother's throat-pouch is a receptacle and protection *only for the hatched-out young ones*.   Should any danger threaten, or when night comes,

---

[1] Jung has here blindly passed over the biological facts, because he seeks to protect himself from the " analytic " tendency to regression, and thereby overlooks the biological.   So he has slipped into the opposite ethical anagogic direction, which places in the centre the idea of rebirth, which is only an intellectualized ramification. *Psychology of the Unconscious*, p. 251.

[2] The brood hatched in the mouth is found in numerous bony fishes, and in isolated cases even among the higher vertebrate animals.   S. Meisenheimer, *Geschlecht und Geschlechter im Tierreich*, Jena, 1921, vol. i., chap. 20; "Die Verwendung des elterlichen Körpers im Dienst der Brutflege," viii., Stufe, p. 566 f.   Here belong also the wonderful homing instincts of birds of passage and migrating fish, which return to *their place of birth* from every strange place to which *they have been taken or to which they themselves have migrated*.

the mother opens her mouth and a whole brood of young Haplochromes creep into it and stay there till the danger is past or the morning dawns. This behaviour is especially interesting, not only because it proves that physiological sleep throughout the whole animal kingdom is a temporary return to the mother's womb but because in this species the real incubation takes place on stones or plants outside the mother's body; this is compensated for later by these animals because they apparently cannot do without it.

Other animals, differing from the pouched animals (kangaroo) in that they have no partial return to the mother's body for protection, replace this in a way that can only be called "symbolic," as, for example, the birds by building their nests[1] (which Jung has already referred to). We want here to draw attention to the fact that what we call animal *instinct* contains in its essence the adjustment of the pre-natal libido to the outer world, and also the tendency to make this outer world resemble as faithfully as possible the previously experienced primal state; whilst man, because of his long period of pregnancy and with the help of later-developed and higher capacities for thought, attempts, in every conceivable way, to re-establish, as it were, creatively the real primal condition. He succeeds in doing this with a great amount of pleasure in the socially adjusted phantasy products of art, religion, mythology; whereas he fails piteously in the neurosis.

The ground for this lies, as Psychoanalysis has shown, in a psycho-biological arrest in development, which we shall discuss in the next chapter from the point of view of the

---

[1] An American kindergarten teacher once told me that little children, when playing with plasticine, mostly spontaneously formed birds' nests.

sexual trauma. The essential factor in the development of neuroses seems to be that man, in the biological as in the cultural overcoming of the birth trauma, which we call adjustment, comes to grief at the cross road of sexual gratification, which most nearly approaches the primal situation, yet does not completely re-establish it in the infantile meaning.

SEXUAL GRATIFICATION

THE whole problem of infantile sex is really contained in the famous question as to the origin of children. This question, to which the child comes sooner or later quite spontaneously, arises, as we have experienced, as the final result of an unsatisfactory process of thought. This can express itself in the child's manifold ways and peculiarities (always asking questions), proving that it seeks in itself for the lost memory of its earlier place of abode, which, in consequence of an extremely intense repression, it cannot find. Hence, as a rule, the child needs some outside stimulus, most frequently the repetition of the experience through the birth of a brother or sister,[1] for the question to express itself openly. And thus the child appeals to the help of grown-up people, who obviously appear to have recovered in some way this lost knowledge. But, as is well known, the mere answering of the child's question, even when done by analytically enlightened educators, brings just as little solution to the child as the communication to an adult neurotic of any of the unconscious causes of his symptoms, which he cannot accept because of similarly unconscious inner resistances and repressions. The child's typical reaction to the truthful answer (the child grows in the mother's body somewhat as the plants grow in the earth) shows also where the real interest of the child lies—namely,

[1] According to various analytic experiences, the only child or the youngest (or also those who have had to repress a severe birth trauma) does not ask the question so directly.

30

in the problem of *how to get inside*. This, however, does not refer so much to the problem of procreation, as adults conclude from themselves, but points rather to the tendency to return to the place where one was before.[1] As the trauma of birth has suffered the most intense repression, the child cannot re-establish the memory of it, in spite of the explanation, and still holds on to its own theories of the origin of children. These manifestly correspond to unconscious reproductions of the pre-natal condition, and leave open the illusion of a possible return which the child would forfeit if it accepted the adult's explanation.

First and foremost is the renowned *fable of the stork*, which seems to have originated for the following reason: that the bird of passage, returning periodically to the same place to fetch a child, can just as well take the child back again with it;[2] whereby, too, the traumatic effect of the plunge into the depths is replaced by the soft even flight of the hardy flier. Another infantile theory of birth, inferred from the Unconscious by Freud, with its reference to the digestive process, links on directly to the mother's womb; the child enters the mother through the mouth (as food) and is ejected as fæces through the rectum. Moreover, this proceeding, which as we know is pleasurable for the child and is daily enacted, would guarantee the ease and possi-

[1] *Mephistopheles:* " 'Tis a law of devils and ghosts:
    Where they crept in, there must they creep out.
    In the first we are free, in the second we have no choice."

Indians, when they weave baskets, etc., do not completely close the circle in the ornamentation, because the women would otherwise bear no children (according to the verbal communication of a traveller).

[2] It may be to other parents (family romance), it may be to the place of its origin (death wish). See the Author's treatise on the *Lohengrin Saga*, 1911.

bility of repetition in the sense of a compensation for the trauma. The later theory, moreover, to which many people cling for a long time, that the child is born by cutting the mother open (generally around the navel), is based on the denial of one's own pains at birth which are then completely imposed on the mother.[1]

The common characteristic of all infantile birth theories, which is also richly illustrated[2] in myths and fairy tales, is the denial of the female sex organ, which clearly shows that it is due to the repression of the birth trauma experienced there. The painful fixation on this function of the female genital as organ of birth lies finally at the bottom of all neurotic disturbances of the adult sex life, of psychical impotence, as of feminine frigidity in all its forms. But it is particularly clearly expressed in certain kinds of phobias (attacks of dizziness), which accompany the feeling that a street is becoming narrower or wider.

Furthermore, *perversions* which, according to Freud, represent the positive side of neuroses, point in different ways to the infantile primal situation. As I have already

[1] Here may be mentioned the typical myth phantasy that the fearless hero is invariably one cut out from the womb, and—usually prematurely—accomplishes, even as a child, wonderful deeds; obviously he is spared the anxiety at birth, and with it also the overcoming of an early neurotic period (see the chapter on " Heroic Compensation," p. 102).

Moreover, from isolated cases, it would seem that children who are brought into the world by means of an operation actually develop better in certain respects. On the other hand, a woman who gave birth to her child while in a narcotic state, felt that it was not hers, because she had not been conscious of its birth. Her infantile interest as to where children really come from has thus remained unsatisfied.

[2] See my treatise: *Völkerpsychologische Parallelen zu den infantilen Sexualtheorien* 1911.

stated elsewhere,[1] the behaviour of a pervert is characterized by the fact that he keeps the infantile anal birth theory from being repressed, by a partial realization of it and by means of the guilt-feeling; he himself plays the part of the anal child before he has to undergo the birth trauma, thus approaching as nearly as possible to the condition of the ('' polymorphous-perverse '') pleasurable primal situation. There is no need of further explanation for *coprolagnia* and *uro-lagnia*. All other kinds of mouth perversions in some way continue[2] the intrauterine libido gratification (or the post-natal gratification at the mother's breast). The *exhibitionist* is characterized by the desire to return into that paradisiacal primal state of nakedness in which he lived before birth, and which the child so loves on that account. A specially keen pleasure is taken, therefore, in the acts of undressing and stripping off coverings, as we find in strongly marked cases. The uncovering of the genitals at the hetero-sexual stage of development corresponds, therefore, to the substitution of the representative part (penis—child) for the whole body, the man preferring the first signification (namely, the penis), the woman the second (child), all of which is connected with the various forms of development of the castration complex (normal feeling of shame). The peculiar characteristic of the sexual shame feeling, shutting or covering of the eyes and blushing,[3]

[1] '' Perversion and Neurosis,'' reprinted from the *International Journal of Psychoanalysis*, vol. iv., Part III., 1923.

[2] From the analysis of a woman who preferred cunnilingus, it appeared that the pleasurable sensation was connected with the feeling of having her clitoris (analogous to the penis) in a warm hole.

[3] The deep connection of the motives of nakedness, dressing, blinding, and chaining (see below) explained by me as '' exhibition-

refers to the pre-natal situation, in which, as is well known, the blood flows to the head in the downward position. The defensive significance, moreover, of exposing the genitals, predominating largely in superstitions, is originally nothing other than an expression of the curse of repression heaped on the organ of birth and clearly shown in the various existing maledictions and curses.

The same applies to *Fetishism*, the mechanism of which Freud long ago described as a partial repression with compensatory substitute formations. The repression quite regularly concerns the mother's genitals in the meaning of the traumatic anxiety-cathexis, and the genitals are replaced by a pleasure-invested part of the body or its æsthetically still more acceptable covering—dresses, shoes, corsets, etc.

Earlier analytic experiences have already allowed me to infer that in masochism it is a question of the conversion of the pains caused by parturition (phantasy of being beaten) into pleasurable sensations.[1] This is explained from other typical elements of masochistic phantasies—for instance, the almost regularly occurring state of being bound (punishment, see later) as a partial reinstatement of the intra-uterine pleasurable condition of immobility, which is

---

istic," first appeared through their common relation to the primal situation (see my treatise, *Die Nacktheit in Sage und Dichtung*, 1911).

[1] Apparently connected with this is the prevalent fertility spell of being beaten with rods (rod of life) as it appears in the myths of the virginal Bona Dea as punishment from her own father, whose desires the chaste goddess resists. One may compare with this the whipping of the bridal pair in the German wedding customs (W. Mannhardt, *Antike Feld-und Wald-kulte*, i., 299-303), in the Roman Lupercalia, and the Mexican festival of Mid-Summer, at which the young girls were beaten with small sacks in order to make them fertile.

apparently only imitated in the widespread custom of binding the baby in swaddling clothes (Sadger).[1] On the other hand, the typical *sadist*, the slayer of children (Gilles de Ray) or murderer of women (Jack the Ripper), who wallows in blood and in bowels, seems completely to play the part of infantile curiosity, and seeks to discover the nature of the inside of the body. Whilst the masochist seeks to re-establish the original pleasurable condition by means of affective revaluation of the birth trauma, the sadist personifies the unquenchable hatred of one who has been expelled; he really attempts with his fully grown body to go back into the place whence he came as a child, without considering that he thereby tears his sacrifice to pieces—this being by no means his main intention (see later about sacrifice, p. 98).

Homosexuality also seems to fit easily into this conception. It is based quite obviously in the case of the man on the abhorrence of the female genitals, and this because of its close relation to the shock of birth. The homosexual sees in woman only the maternal organ of birth, and hence is incapable of acknowledging it as an organ for giving pleasure. Moreover, as we know from analyses, the homosexuals of both sexes only consciously play the part of man and woman. Unconsciously they invariably play the part of *mother and child*—which is directly manifest in the case of female homosexuality—and so far actually represent a special kind of love relationship ("the third sex"), namely, a direct

[1] In the last-mentioned forms (exhibitionism, masochism) the especially prominent part played by the "skin, mucous membrane, and muscle erotism," so called by Sadger, seems directly deducible from the intrauterine position, where the whole body is, so to say, pleasantly tickled by a snug feeling of softness, warmth, and fluidity.

continuance of the asexual but libidinal binding of the primal situation. It is worth emphasizing the fact that homosexuality, being that perversion which apparently relates only to the differentiation of sex, really rests, as a whole, on the bisexuality of the embryonal condition surviving in the Unconscious.[1]

These considerations take us straight to the heart of the problem of sexuality, which later submits the simple manifestations of the primal libido to such complicated and unlooked-for changes. I think that by adhering to the conception we have been elaborating, we shall gain a better understanding of normal sexual development, and overcome the apparent difficulties.

It has been noticed, especially in recent times, that our whole mental outlook has given predominance to the man's point of view and has almost entirely neglected the woman's. The clearest example of this one-sidedness both of social and scientific thought is possibly the fact that long and important periods of the development of human culture stood under the sway of the so-called mother right (" discovered " by Bachofen). These periods were under the rule of the woman, and obviously special efforts in overcoming resistances had first to be made in order to accept as facts these periods which had been " repressed " even from the traditions themselves.[2] How far this attitude survives even in psychoanalysts is shown in the fact that, as a rule, we tacitly represent the sexual relations only from

---

[1] This shows the weakness of Adler's " masculine protest " as a principle for the elucidation of perversion (homosexuality).

[2] See M. Vaerting, *Die weibliche Eigenart im Männerstaat und die männliche Eigenart im Frauenstaat*, Karlsruhe, 1921.

the man's point of view, ostensibly on account of its simplicity, but if we are more honest, from an insufficient understanding of the woman's sexual life. I hardly think that this attitude is the consequence of a social under-estimation of woman, as Alfred Adler thinks, but the reverse. Both are the expression of that primal repression which tries to degrade and to deny woman both socially and intellectually on account of her original connection with the birth trauma. In attempting to make conscious again the repressed primal memory of the birth trauma, we believe that we shall reinstate the high estimation of woman which was repressed simultaneously with the birth trauma, and we can do this by freeing her from the weight of the curse on her genitals.

We have learnt with astonishment from the analyses accomplished by Freud that there is a valid, although intensely repressed, masculine counterpart to the girl's envy of the penis, already familiar to superficial observation. This is the boy's unconscious wish to be able to bear children through the anus. This wish-phantasy, which through the unconscious identification of child and fæces (anal child), later of child and penis, remains active in the Unconscious, likewise represents nothing other than an attempt to re-establish the primal situation in which one was still an " anal " child. But this is before one has learnt to know the female genitals, the primary perception of which remains physiologically certain, but which psychologically is represented, for the first time, by the birth trauma. That the boy, soon after birth, presupposes his own member in all other beings, is indeed easily intelligible from the anthropomorphic attitude of man in general. Nevertheless, the obstinacy with which he clings to this conception, against all appearances, should warn us not to credit this to his narcissistic self over-estimation alone. It is much more probable to assume, that, for as long as possible, the boy wants to deny the existence of the female genitals, because he wishes to avoid being reminded of the horror of passing this organ, which still haunts him in every member. In other words, he does not want to reproduce the anxiety-affect connected with his birth. As a proof of this, however, it seems to me that the little girl has the same negative attitude towards her own genitals, precisely because they are the female organs, and she cannot share in the narcissistic advantage of possessing a penis. This attitude is manifested in the so-called " envy of the penis," which shows, moreover, that the chief part is by no means played by the more or less conscious motivation of the Ego (envy). On the contrary, it is proved that both sexes attempt, in the same way, to deny and disregard the female genitals, because both, regardless of sex, are subjected to the primal repression of the mother's genitals. In both, the over-estimation of the penis—explained by Adler in conformance with his academic sex-psychology from the feeling of " inferiority," which is not even a secondary feeling—finally proves to be a reaction formation against the existence in general of female sex organs from which one was once painfully thrust out. The acceptance of " castration " as a normal condition of female development, but one which we also see typically expressed in the masculine neurotic's wish for castration, is well fitted, in consequence of the already mentioned phantastic element, to replace the actual separation from the mother, by identification with her, and thus indirectly, through sexual love, to approach once more to the primal situation.

For, as Ferenczi[1] has ingeniously shown, the man, penetrating into the vaginal opening, undoubtedly signifies a partial return to the womb, which by identification with the penis known as a symbol for a child (Tom Thumb, German *Däumling*) becomes not only a complete but also an infantile return. But in the case of the woman, the attitude is quite similar, as analytic material has shown. By means of the clitoris libido, experienced so intensely in masturbation, the woman is able—often only too able— to identify herself with the penis or the man and so indirectly to approach the return into the womb. The tendency to apparent masculinity revealed in it rests on the unconscious identification with the father and finally aims at becoming, at least a participator in the inestimable advantage which the man has over the woman, and which consists in his being able partially to go back into the mother, by means of the penis, itself representing the child. For the woman there results a still more far-reaching and normal gratification of this primal wish manifesting itself as mother love in the identification with the fruit of the body.

Two facts analytically revealed are able to explain the unconscious equivalence of child and penis, which we so frequently find to be conscious in psychoses. First, as described by Boehm (*Zschr.*, viii., 1922), the (homosexual or impotent) man's frequent fear of an enormous " active " penis (like a sort of trunk or horse's penis), hidden in the woman and suddenly flung out, clearly refers to the identification with the child who is hidden inside the maternal genitals, and suddenly, in parturition, comes out. The feminine counterpart to this idea, of a " woman with a penis," was

---

[1] " Versuch einer Genitaltheorie " (Congress, report), *Zschr.*, viii. 1922, p. 479.

given to me from analyses, especially of frigidity in women. It was not, as one might expect, the first sight of a little boy's (a brother's or playmate's) member that had a pathological influence in the sense of the "penis-envy." But rather was it the sight of a *large* (erected or paternal) genital organ that had the traumatic effect, because it was a reminder of the size of the child. Thus, instead of the entrance, perceived (through masturbation) on one's own body, it showed that there is already something hidden inside, which obstructs the presumed entrance, and later (at the sexual stage) manifests itself, as something which will enter one's own body (compare with this the fear of small animals). The often conscious fright of neurotic women as to how the large organ shall go into them rests indirectly on the primal repression of the birth trauma. On the other hand, woman's well-known high estimation of a large penis shows that through this and even on account of this there is found the greatest possibility of pleasure, which sometimes can be increased through possible pains in the sense of the primal situation. From the analyses of feminine frigidity (vaginismus) it became certain that the typical (masochistic) phantasies of being violated or raped, which are repressed in these women, represent nothing else than a failure in their attempt to adjust themselves to their (feminine) sexual part, because these phantasies prove to be the precipitate of the initial identification with the man (penis), which should make possible the aggressive-libidinal entering into the mother.[1] The masculine prototype to this we find in (for most men) the especially pleasurable (sadistic), act of defloration, with its painful and bloody

[1] Compare with this typical form of feminine object choice, my work already mentioned on the libido-processes in the cure (*l.c.*).

penetration of the female genitals into which no one has yet entered.[1]

Thus, in the first stage of childhood, both sexes behave in the same way towards the primal object of their libido, the mother. The conflict which we see so impressively revealed in neuroses occurs first of all with the knowledge of sex differences, which for both sexes alike represents the decisive trauma for later formation of neuroses. For the boy, because he has learnt to recognize the female genitals, from which he originated and into which later he has to enter; for the girl, because she has learnt to recognize the masculine genitals, which not only seem to make an entrance into the love-object impossible for her, but which later are even destined to enter forcibly her own body. If the girl successfully overcomes this trauma by a fortunate adjustment to the Œdipus situation, then, in later love life, through the sexual act, she comes to a partial gratification of the primal wish, or, at any rate, to as far-reaching a satisfaction as is possible. The coming to grief at this trauma is, however, decisive for later neuroses, in which the Œdipus and cas-

---

[1] Compare also the later references to mythological material (p. 110). It would seem, moreover, that these unconscious strivings, as so many others, exist in folklore as facts not yet understood. For example, the Australian aborigines' well-known operation, which is carried out mostly after circumcision (between the ages of twelve and fourteen years), and which produces an artificial hypospadias which makes the penis, in the erected state, flat and lobe-shaped. In women—whose labia and clitoris are frequently cut in order not to harm the children (obviously in birth)—the hymen is forcibly cut to make coitus possible, and the vaginal entrance is widened by a cut towards the anus. Nevertheless, the man introduces his penis still with great difficulty, obviously from the fear of getting stuck or completely falling in. (For details about the operations, see Reitzenstein's already mentioned article in *Handwörterbuch der Sexualwissenschaft*, p. 5 ff.)

tration complexes play so astonishing a part, and in which in both sexes the aversion to sexuality stands in the foreground. Both, then, are thrown back into neurosis at the stage of the first genital conflict, and from there flee further back into the original libido situation, which again for both sexes consists of a return to the mother.

The man can from the beginning remain attached to the same object, which represents for him, mother, lover, and wife. The father then soon becomes the representative of the anxiety connected with the mother (the mother's genitals). In the case of the woman, on the other hand, it is necessary to transfer a part of the original mother libido to the father, which is parallel to the movement to passivity already estimated by Freud. It is a matter, then, for the girl to give up all idea of an active return to the mother, a penetration which is recognized or imagined to be the masculine privilege, and in the supreme joy of motherhood, to be content with the wish to regain the blessed primal state by means of passive reproduction—that is, by means of pregnancy and the birth of her own child. The failure of this psycho-biological metamorphosis is to be seen in female neurotics, who, without exception, reject the man's genitals, and in the sense of the so-called " masculine complex " want the penis only as an instrument for their own penetration into the love-object. Thus both sexes become neurotic, when they wish to gratify the primal libido for the mother, as compensation for the birth trauma, not by means of the sexual gratification designed for them, but by means of the original form of infantile gratification, whereby they again inevitably stumble upon the anxiety-borders of the birth trauma, which are best to be avoided just by means of sexual gratification.

Sexual love, then, which reaches its climax in the mating of two beings, proves to be the most sublime attempt partially to re-establish the primal situation between mother and child, which only finds its complete realization in a new embryo.   And when Plato explains the essence of love as the yearning of two parts which, formerly united, have become severed, he gives poetical utterance to the supreme[1] biological attempt to overcome the birth trauma, by the genuine " platonic love," that of the child for the mother.

On the strength of this concept it is somewhat easier to understand the development of the sexual instinct, which in opposition to the libido is still condemned to " procreation " as the only means of final gratification.   The first clear expression of the sexual instinct is manifest in the *Œdipus complex*, the connection of which with the wish to return to the mother's womb has been interpreted by Jung in the sense of the anagogic "rebirth phantasy," whereas Ferenczi (as quoted above) has rehabilitated it as the latter's biological foundation.   At the back of the Œdipus saga there really stands the mysterious question of the origin and destiny of man, which Œdipus desires to solve, not intellectually, but by actually returning into the mother's womb.[2]   This happens entirely in a symbolic form, for his blindness in the deepest sense represents a return into the darkness of the mother's womb, and his final disappearance through a cleft rock into the Underworld expresses once again the same wish tendency to return into the mother earth.

[1] One can compare with this the Biblical expression: " Man and woman are one flesh," etc. (Erant duo in carne uno).

[2] The vaginal symbolism of the ravine (or three ways) in the Œdipus saga, recently shown up by Abraham, recurs in the well-known intrauterine phantasy into which the father (or his penis) disturbingly enters (see *Imago*, ix., 1923, p. 124 ff.).

We are now in a position to understand the psycho-biological meaning of the Œdipus complex, as manifested in normal development. From the standpoint of the birth trauma, we have in the Œdipus complex a glimpse of the first valuable attempt to overcome the anxiety or fear of the (mother's) genitals, by being able to accept them in a pleasurable way as libido-object. In other words, this is to transfer the original, *i.e.*, intrauterine, possibility of pleasure to the genital outlet which is charged with anxiety, and there to reopen a former source of pleasure buried by repression. The first attempt is from the very beginning condemned to failure, not only because it is undertaken with an imperfectly developed sexual apparatus, but chiefly because the attempt is made upon the primal object itself, with which the entire anxiety and repression of the primal trauma is directly connected. But this also explains why this (one is inclined to say) "still-born" attempt has to be made at all. Obviously, it is a necessary condition for success of the later normal transference in the love-choice that the child should repeat the separation from the primal object at the first stage of its sexual development as a *sexual trauma*. But this also condemns the Œdipus complex, as the third important repetition of the primal trauma of separation, to be drawn down to Oreus by the primal repression of the birth trauma, only to go on reacting with the typical relapse-symptoms at every new libido privation.

We are therefore of opinion that the inception of sexual development, which according to Freud occurs twice, is made intelligible from the history of the individual, because we recognize in it the reminiscence of the conditions so deeply sundered by the trauma of birth—the pleasurable intra-uterine life and the difficulties in adaptation to the extrauterine world. The "latency-period" then follows the sexual trauma of the severance from the mother on the sexual level (Œdipus complex). During the latency period there occurs a temporary renunciation of direct regressive tendencies in favour of adjustment, till, at puberty, is reached the primacy of the genital zone which, in the meaning of our arguments, we must think of as a *regaining* of the appreciation of the (mother's) genitals, once experienced as primal object of value. For the genital primacy, which, by means of the (male) genitals, signifies the final substitution of the whole body as object in place of the mother, can only be admitted when the primal and painful experience connected with the genitals has successfully been changed back into the nearest possible approach to the pleasure experienced inside the mother as one's original abode. The possibility for this is provided under the extensive disturbance known as puberty, culminating in the act of love with its many phases and variations, all of which tend towards a contact as intimate as possible (to eat for love) (*L'animal a deux dos*). It is therefore not without cause that the state of being in love, which can go as far as identifying the whole outer world with the object of affection (Wagner's *Tristan and Isolde*), has been described as a neurotic introversion, and coitus with its momentary loss of consciousness as a slight hysterical attack.

NEUROTIC REPRODUCTION

AFTER having followed the development of the child's libido up to the sexual trauma of the Œdipus complex and recognized in it the decisive point for the formation of neuroses, we can return to the question as to how far each neurotic symptom, as it becomes intelligible in the analytic process of healing, conforms to the birth trauma. The formula seems to be quite simple: analysis, as is well known, has proved *anxiety* to be the nucleus of every neurotic disturbance, and as we know through Freud that the primal anxiety lies in the birth trauma, the connection with it should be everywhere as easy to prove as it is in the case of the child's emotional reactions. The point, however, is not merely that the anxiety-*affect*, which then attaches itself in various forms to definite contents, originates in that primal source, but that in analysis isolated symptoms and the whole neurosis formation point quite definitely to reproduced reminiscences of birth or of the pleasurable stage preceding it. If finally we turn to the original " traumatic " theory of neuroses, as it was formulated in the classical *Studien über Hysterie* more than twenty-five years ago, I think that neither we nor the originator of this theory need feel ashamed of it. Indeed, one might say that in all these years of analytic investigation, rich in results and experiences, none of us—even after taking all other factors into consideration—has abandoned the certainty that there is still more in the " trauma " than we trust ourselves to admit. In any case, we must admit as justifiable the doubt in the activity

46

of those apparent traumata which Freud early recognized as mere repetitions of " primal-phantasies," the psycho-biological foundation of which we now believe to have found in the universal human trauma of birth with all its consequences.

We can trace this becoming neurotic *in statu nascendi* as a short circuit, so to say, in the real *traumatic neurosis*, especially as it was observed during the war (war neurosis). There the primal anxiety is directly mobilized through shock, the otherwise unconsciously reproduced birth situation being affectively materialized through the outer danger of death.[1] The fundamental significance of the birth trauma as a means of expressing every neurotic anxiety is proved by the fact that it forms the starting-point of the most diverse neurotic symptoms which in other cases can arise without the operation of a shock. But the traumatic neurosis with this particular combination of form and content stands at the beginning of a pathogenic series, whereas the straightforward pyschoneuroses, the content of which is determined by the sexual trauma, stand at the end. The latter avail themselves of the same universal expression of regression as a means of defence and as an outlet as soon as the individual in some way or other comes to grief in Reality. The neurotic, generally speaking, as analysis has proved, fails in sexuality; which in this connection is as good as saying that he is not content with the gratification of partially returning to the mother, afforded in the sexual act and in the child, but has remained fixedly " infantile " and even still desires to go *completely* or as a

[1] The dreams of patients with " traumatic " neuroses " repeat " in typical ways the birth trauma in the form of an actual traumatic experience, but mostly with some betraying detail of birth.

whole back into the mother. Finally, he is incapable of settling the birth trauma in the normal way by preventing anxiety through sexual gratification, and is thrown back to the primal form of libido gratification which remains unattainable and against which his adult Ego strives by developing anxiety.

At various points in our discussions about the development of the child's libido, the corresponding phenomena of the neurosis have incidentally been shown, especially in conditions in which anxiety is manifest, just as in the direct disturbances of the sexual function ("actual neurosis"). To give us a better understanding of neurotic anxiety conditions, let us once again recall the simplest case of the release of childish anxiety, which remains typical for every neurotic release of anxiety—namely, the anxiety shown by the child left alone in a dark room. This situation—one can scarcely express it in any other way, although it is not entirely so— "reminds" the child's Unconscious of the dark abode in the mother's womb, which at that time, indeed, was an experience of extreme pleasure—thus explaining the tendency to re-establish it—but which was brought to an end by the frightening severance from the mother, whom now the child misses when alone. In the fear of being alone the child is obviously reminded (er-innert) of the anxiety-affect of the first separation from the libido-object, indeed by an actual re-experience, by the process of reproduction and discharge. This compulsion to the reproduction of a strong painful affect, the mechanism of which we shall discuss later, illustrates, at any rate, the validity and reality of this "reminiscence." All forms of the neurotic development of anxiety, including phobias, conform to the same process, according to the mechanism revealed through analysis. The same may be said of the so-called actual form of anxiety neurosis, which like neurasthenia can be traced to direct disturbances of the sexual function, since the coitus-interruptus causing it corresponds to the anxiety roused by the mother's genitals (dangerous *vagina dentata*). All forms of masculine impotence—the penis being scared away from going in—and all forms of feminine anæsthesia (vaginismus) rest in the same way on the primal fixation on the mother and on infantile anxiety as we have described it. Here, according to the hysterical mechanism described by Freud, the one function of the organ is renounced in favour of another unconscious one; pleasure-function versus bearing-function, wherein lies the opposition between the species (propagation) and the individual (pleasure).[1]

These pronounced symptoms of anxiety show that the neurotic has overcome the birth trauma only in a highly insufficient degree. The physical symptoms of *hysteria*, not only in their manifest forms but also in their deepest unconscious content, show various directly physical reproductions of birth with the pronounced tendency to deny it, that is, to return into the previous pleasure situation of the intrauterine life. To this category belong pre-eminently the phenomena of hysterical *paralysis*, of which, for example, the inhibited function of walking or moving is nothing other than the physically materialized agoraphobia,[2] while the

---

[1] See the corresponding arguments in my work entitled " Perversion and Neurosis," *Internat. Journal of Psychoanalysis*.

[2] *Cf.* Federn's work (*Jahrb.*, vi., 1914), "Über zwei typische Traumsensationen," of inhibition and flying, as well as their relation to the neurotic symptoms of paralysis or of dizziness. All these sensations prove to be unambiguous reproductions of corresponding sensations at birth (see in the chapter " Symbolic Adaptation " what is said about the dream, p. 78).

immobility brings to realization at the same time the pleasurable primal situation, with the dread or horror of being freed therefrom. The typical phenomena of paralysis, characterized by the drawing in of the extremities to the body, just as the disturbance of co-ordination, seen for example in *chorea minor*, approach even more faithfully to the intrauterine position.[1]

When we give foundation to these hysterical symptoms as being reproductions of the intrauterine state, or of birth, the problem of *conversion* also appears in a new light. What needs to be explained is, not the " conversion " of psychical excitations into physical, but how means of expression which were purely physical in origin could come to demand psychical expression. But this demand appears to be the mechanism by which the *anxiety* arises, which is, so to say, *the first psychical content* of which the human being is conscious. From anxiety to the further psychical superstructure many ways lead, of which we will follow the culturally, as also pathologically, most important under the name of symbol formation. Here we want only briefly to allude to phantasy formations, those psychical offshoots of hysterical physical symptoms, as expressed for example in the so-called hysterical dream or twilight states (including loss of consciousness). From Abraham's (*Jahrb.*, ii., 1910) excellent description it is obvious that in them it is a matter of " psychical conversions "—*i.e.*, of reproductions of the primal situation in the *psychical* sphere—whereby the physical return to the mother is replaced by the mere introversion of the libido. Withdrawal from the outer world is represented by psychical isolation, which we see then materialized

---

[1] One sees how this concept links on to Meynert's, who already traced the movements of *chorea minor* to the movements of the suckling.

in psychoses. Moreover, it is characteristic of these dream states that they frequently end with the affect of anxiety, which sets a limit to regression in the phantasy, as anxiety often does to the night dream. How near these states approach to mystical ecstasies and inner meditations is well known, although their origin is not understood.[1]

Further, all neurotic disturbances in breathing (asthma), which repeat the feeling of suffocation, relate directly to the physical reproductions of the birth trauma. The extensive use of the neurotic headache (migraine) goes back to the specially painful part allotted to the head in parturition, and ultimately all attacks of convulsions noticeable in quite small children, even in the new-born, can be regarded as a directly continued attempt to get rid of the primal birth trauma. Finally, the great hysterical attack uses the same mechanism, occurring, as it does, at the full height of sexual development, and showing a complete defence mechanism in the well known *arc de cercle* position, which is diametrically opposed to the doubled-up embryonal position.[2]

[1] Cavendish Moxon (" Mystical Ecstasy and Hysterical Dream States," *Journal of Abnormal Psychology*, 1920-21, p. 329) describes the relation to ecstasy, while Theodore Schroeder (" Pre-natal Psychism and Mystical Pantheism," *Internat. Journal of Psychoanalysis*, vol. iii., 1922), in his more fundamental work, alludes to the pre-natal factors.

[2] This entire conception, perhaps, contains a reference to the deeper significance of Hysteria as " uterus "-disease (see also Eisler, *Hysterische Erscheinungen am Uterus*, Kongress-vortrag, Berlin, September, 1922).
Also the typical menstrual difficulties can be easily understood in this sense, as birth is actually only a menstruation *en masse*. Menstruation, which also " periodically " continues the womb existence, seems to have been drawn into the general repression of the birth trauma by our civilization. Originally the sign of the woman's extremely desirable ability to become pregnant, it has become, with repression, the meeting-point of the most various neurotic disturbances.

Starting from the hysterical attack which Psychoanalysis has recognized as the equivalent of and defence against the position of coitus, let us touch upon some problems of the mechanism and choice of neuroses. The eminent aversion to sexuality, so clearly to be seen in hysterical attacks, is a consequence of the mother fixation. The female patient denies in " organ speech " simultaneously with the sexual wish, also the wish to return to the womb, which prevents her from accepting the normal sexual adjustment. This pathological sexualization of parturition is the caricature of the normal sexualization necessary for the attainment of the heterosexual aim. On the other hand, the whole quantum of sexual desire (libido) is, so to say, transferred from later development back again to the infantile primal situation, a fact which gives to the attack that lustful character described by so many observers. One could formulate the hysterical attack, translated into conscious language, as a cry " Away from the (mother's) genitals !" and indeed in the sexual as well as in the infantile sense. But the same mechanism is shown also in all other hysterical " displacements " (made intelligible by analysis), which mostly tend towards the upper half of the body (displacement upwards), whereby it may be not without importance, that the head is the first to leave the mother's genitals, and is therefore that part of the body which not merely experiences the birth trauma the most intensely, but is also the first to pass it.

From particular analyses, one gets the definite impression that the later " choice " of the *form* of neurosis is determined quite decisively by the process of birth, the special point of attack of the trauma,[1] and the individual's reaction to

[1] *Cf.* with this the typical physical deformities of new-born heroes, p. 106.

it. Without wishing to anticipate detailed investigations, I would like to formulate the general impression that displacement both above (*globus—dyspnœa*) and below (paralysis — cramps) corresponds in every case to a divergence from the genitals as a centre. This point of view is of paramount importance for the understanding of the neurotic type of character in general and its entire method of reaction, as it embraces the psycho-biological reactions to the birth trauma in their entirety. Thus, the physical symptoms, mostly by evading the border of anxiety, attempt to regress directly into the pre-natal stage, so that the anxiety, evaded either directly or according to the above mentioned (p. 19) form of defence on the part of the Ego, is manifested as sexual guilt-feeling. This would explain the sexual significance of such symptoms as, for example, stiffness, reddening, erection. From the same point of anxiety— viz., the mother's genital-exit-and-entrance, the psychical symptoms attempt to approach the same goal in the opposite direction to the psycho-physical apparatus, by means of phantasy formation, introversion, hallucination, and the stuporous and katatonic twilight states understood as the final stage of this series. Both ways lead finally to the so-called " sexual disinclination," which ultimately goes back to the aversion to the mother's genitals; the physical symptoms of displacement and conversion accomplish this in allowing the genitals to be replaced by a substitute for the genitals less invested with anxiety; the psychical symptoms, by at first attempting to lead away and to turn aside from the physical in general, give rise to the processes of sublimation and reaction formations, which we then see expressed in the highest forms of developed accomplishments, such as Art, Philosophy, and Ethics.

To have recognized and investigated in detail these widely branched psychical connections is the undisputed merit of Psychoanalysis today. On the other hand, it still lacked a firmly-established foundation for the psychical " meaning " of *physical* symptoms. But now we believe that our concept of the birth trauma in its psycho-biological importance is able to fill up these gaps, because it recurs to a state which gives us for the first time, so to say, a real substratum for all psycho-physiological connections and relations. The conception outlined in Ferenczi's[1] studies of hysteria and made valid for organic diseases by Groddeck,[2] seems to me to maintain its real biological foundation only through the full theoretical valuation of the birth trauma. From the reproduction in dreams of the birth and intrauterine situations it is only a step to the corresponding manifestations in hysteria, and from there again only a step to similar purely organic disease symptoms, which always seem to have the same " meaning " and to serve similar tendencies. The transition of these different forms of phenomena into one another is so fluid, that sometimes it is scarcely possible to form any diagnostic differentiation. In tracing these phenomena back to a primal state, where the psycho-physical is still united, where no separation has yet taken place (Groddeck), not only the mechanism but also the form and content of neurotic physical symptoms become intelligible. This is valid for cases recognized as " psychical " just as much as for those qualified as neurologic or organic. From the standpoint of our concept it is a matter of in-difference whether an anatomic lesion of the brain, or a

---

[1] *Hysterie und Pathoneurosen*, 1919.

[2] *Psychische Bedingtheit und psychoanalytische Behandlung organischer Leiden*, 1917. Also *Das Buch vom Es*.

toxic irritation, or lastly a purely psychogenetic experience compels the Ego to give in to the eternal pressure of the Unconscious and to regress to the primal source of libido gratification and protection. The similarity of the symptoms from these different causes then becomes obvious; all the artificial setting up of problems disappears, for the individual can do nothing but go back as far along the channels of psycho-physical development as the individual fixation of anxiety and the limits of repression respectively will allow. A problem would arise only if the symptoms were not so similar as they actually are and must necessarily be.

I must be content here with referring to a few striking examples, and must leave the further pursuit of these highly suggestive explanations to experienced neurologists and internal specialists. Thus cases of *narcolepsy*, genuine as well as hysteroid, manifest the typical condition of the embryonal sleep; in these cases the symptom of sudden paralysis of the will, cataleptic inhibitions, might turn out to have a biological relation to this fœtal state (position of the limbs). It does not seem accidental that the sudden desire for sleep overtakes the patient just in dangerous situations (when crossing a street or travelling by rail, etc.); which again reminds one of the somnambulists who love to put themselves in positions which, under normal conditions, would be the cause of fear. In the parallel organic disease, encephalitis, the well-known symptoms of changing day into night, dyspnœa, and tics, seem to refer directly to the birth trauma. The practical importance of this insight is given by linking it on to the well-known clinical experience of how easily these and similar conditions can be psychically influenced.[1]

[1] I refer here to Paul Schilder's remark made at the time of writing this work (April, 1923) which showed that attacks of

There is, however, no doubt that just as the same symptom can originate from either side, it must also be possible to influence it therapeutically from both sides. When recently there was some talk of attacks of asthma—even such as were of a psychic nature—having been influenced favourably by operating on the larynx, similar recent experiences of the removal of nervous phenomena in children (such as anxiety states and dreams, etc.), by freeing the nasal passages, admitted of just as little doubt.[1] On the other hand, through the knowledge of the psychophysical mechanism at work in these cases, one will not be surprised to hear that children who have been under anæsthetics develop some time later direct states of anxiety, which apparently they had long ago overcome. Nor ought we to be surprised to hear that, after an anæsthetic, existing states of anxiety (of sleeping alone in a dark room, anxiety dreams, nightmares, etc.), occur in greatly intensified form.[2] All these facts may be explained by saying that the physical symptoms (for instance, striving for breath) automatically mobilize the birth anxiety and the entire psychical complex connected

chorea minor, for example, disappear as soon as one puts the patient to bed, and which also emphasized the ease with which senile states of abasia and astasia can be psychically influenced.

[1] See Dr. Stein in the *Wiener Klin. Wochenschrift* (April, 1923) and the simultaneous communications (in the *Gesellschaft der Ärzte zu Wien*) by Eppinger (Klinik Wenckebach) and Hofer (Klinik Hajek) concerning treatment by operation in cases of *angina pectoris*.

[2] To an English child specialist I owe the report that children, after having their tonsils operated on under a narcotic, for years after often have attacks of nightly anxiety, which have been traced even by the parents themselves (or other observers) to the trauma of the operation. Moreover, this is according to individual experiences quite frequent among grown-up people, who react to operations under anæsthetics with typical dreams or symptoms symbolizing regression to the mother.

with it, or that the narcotic sleep goes back again to the primal situation. It will depend on the kind and severity of the case whether one will determine for it an organic (operative) or psychical treatment. The latter at present is still too unfamiliar, but sooner or later it will be adopted with appropriate simplification.

Finally, one should mention in this connection a problem which seems of general importance. If, for instance, we consistently carry through the analysis of a compulsion neurosis, we note it as a first success, when we have enabled the patient to go back from his purely intellectual speculations to the early infantile stages of the neurosis—namely, to the compulsive actions and eventually even to the original pleasurable actions. Quite frequently even physical " conversion " symptoms are thereby renewed. Analysis then shows that the compulsion neurosis frequently—my limited experience prevents me from saying always, although I have regularly found it so—issues from an hysterical kernel, which we must assume as the foundation of every child's neurosis.

And as one can almost invariably discover an hysterical nucleus, directly dependent on the birth trauma in the background of the compulsion neurosis, so the analysis of some hysterical cases has taught me that, besides the disposition to physical symptoms (" conversion ") existing since earliest childhood (severe birth trauma) and tumultuously pressing forward into a neurosis, there is nearly always a vein of neurotic compulsion running through the hysterical primal stratum. Without discovering this, a completed analysis of hysteria and the removal of its symptoms remain impossible. In cases which I remember of hysteria in women, it was quite clear that the physical symptoms, based on the birth trauma, were almost completely used to express the (heterosexual) Œdipus complex: thus they could be traced back to the transference of the libido to the father, the reaction to disappointment, and subsequent guilt-feeling. Physical symptoms of the neurosis in women patients thus prove to be a sediment of the libido pathologically displaced on to the father (mother identification).

At the disillusionment in the father a part of the girl's libido turns back to the mother, in order to enjoy again the earliest libido fixation which had been partially given up (transferred to the father). As this is doomed to fail, because the mother in the meantime has become a rival in the Œdipus situation, a yet stronger means of defence must now be seized in order to complete the final liberation from the mother which is biologically necessary. This occurs by the means, discovered through analysis, of converting love into hate, which is the characteristic mechanism for the compulsion neurosis. But this hate, which should serve the purpose of setting the individual free from the binding love to the mother, signifies only another kind of fixation to the mother to whom one is now bound by hate. The secondary attempts to become free mostly occur under the traumatic impression of a newly born brother or sister, and lead to the displacement of the affect on to the infant, or to the father, who is the real cause of separation from the mother. Here is to be sought the main root of the " death wish " (in women patients) for the mother, which attempts to overcome their own longing to return by getting rid of the mother. Further ways of forming reactions to this " sadistic " death wish not compatible with the Ego are already analytically understood and valued in detail from the ethical inhibitions (hyper-morality, compassion) to the most severe self-punishment (masochism, depression).

The attempts which recur in such exaggerated form in compulsive thoughts and ponderings to master this ambivalent primal conflict through intellectual work belong to the later decisive period of the child's sexual "interest." In pulling down this speculative superstructure, which we accomplish by releasing anxiety and by freeing libido, we are really driving the primal anxiety, entrenched in the system and scarcely discoverable, back again into the physical, in order to disperse it in this normal way—by conducting it, as it were, to earth.

This process, likewise moving along psychobiological channels, can now work itself off in a normal measure under less extreme conditions. And one actually has the impression, from very many purely organic sufferings, that they save the individual—if one may so express it—from the luxury of a neurosis formation. But it would be more correct to say that the neurosis is a more pretentious substitute for a banal organic suffering, both of which have at bottom the same cause. One is not infrequently astonished to see how it is precisely a neurosis, with its " counterfeit " physical symptoms, that prevents the development of any real disease of the same organ, just because it is a substitute for it. Moreover, it is also remarkable—as Freud incidentally mentions—that patients who, for example, have suffered many years from the severest attacks of anxiety, yet look flourishing, just as patients who suffer for years from sleeplessness do not become so exhausted as individuals who "really" have not slept for a long time. Obviously the Unconscious gets so much primal libido from the symptom that it makes up for the "neurotic" deficiency.

From hysterical phenomena in the extremities, which characteristically go back to the complex of the primal trauma, we are led directly to certain ceremonial and compulsive positions in bed, such as we can observe in young children and in certain obsessional patients, who also insist upon meticulous arrangements of their clothes. That this ceremonial is related to the position in bed is in harmony with our conception of sleep as being a temporary return to the embryonal situation.

Without considering the forms of transition from hysterical symptoms to obsessional actions, for example, the tics, etc.,[1] we want to lay stress only on the classical obsessional neurosis, in which the way from the original physical symptoms (obsessional actions) to the purely psychical and, indeed, intellectual attempt at mastery, has been completely cleared up by analysis. If what has been said about hysteria is completely valid for the physical phenomena (*i.e.*, tics) of the obsessional neurotic, so the typical obsessional thoughts and ponderings, as shown by analysis, go back to the infantile problem concerning the origin of children, and link on to the first childish attempt *intellectually to master the birth trauma*. The obsessional neurotic, therefore, finally succeeds by means of the " omnipotence of thought " in getting back to the longed-for primal situation (Ferenczi).[2] He accomplishes this indirectly, however, in his individual way by plunging into philosophic speculations about death and immortality as well as the " beyond " and its eternal punishment. In this way he repeats the seemingly unavoid-

---

[1] Here also belong the so-called "impulse actions " (Stekel), which are obsessional actions mostly performed in (hysterical) twilight states (migratory instinct: homesickness—" going back "; pyromania: fire—warmth—mother).

[2] *Contributions to Psychoanalysis*, p. 181.

able projection of life before birth into the future after death. This projection made by mankind for many thousands of years in the entangled bypaths of mistaken religious superstitions, and crowned by the doctrine of immortality, still continues to exist today in the widespread, intense interest in the supernatural, and in occultism with its world of spirits.[1]

The changes of moods in obsessional neurotics are closely related to circular insanity (cyclothymia), whereas their speculative system formation is closely related to certain pronounced forms of psychoses. Circular insanity, with its sudden changes from melancholy to mania, goes directly back to the reproduction of sensations before and after birth, in that the primal mechanism of change from pleasure to pain at the loss of the first libido object, namely, the severance from the womb, is repeated over and over again. The form of disease is therefore of quite special importance for the study of the pleasure-pain problem. In analyses of deep states of depression, one is able to crystallize the libido consumed therein, so to speak, as a precipitate. The libido then often expresses itself, as one patient put it, as " a sexual excitement over the whole surface of the body." The melancholic stage, which is so aptly called " depression," is characterized by physical symptoms, all of which tend to regress to the intrauterine position.[2] The emotion of grief

[1] I cannot here refrain from quoting a characteristic expression of Thomas Mann, who in describing a spiritualistic séance at Schrenck-Nötzing's at which he was present, gave his impression of the medium, etc. (in a lecture in Vienna on March 29, 1923). " The situation gave a mystical impression simply through the struggling for breath of the medium, whose state decisively and unambiguously reminds one of parturition."

[2] A bent carriage of the body, curling up in bed, lying without movement and speech for days at a time, refusal to feed oneself, etc.

or sorrow expresses the fact that *post natum omne animal triste est*. The manic stage frequently following the depressive is physically distinguished, on the other hand, by the post-natal liveliness and movement, whilst the feeling of extreme happiness and blessedness conforms to the pre-natal libido gratification. We will explain the interesting mechanism of this peculiarly alternating distribution of affect and content in discussing the pleasure-pain mechanism (see pp. 187 and 199). Here where it is only a question of briefly mentioning this new point of view, we must refrain from showing how the finer details of symptom formation or the mechanism of the distribution of affect can be understood purely analytically in the meaning of our concept. The symptomatic conformation of the pre-natal and post-natal libido situation becomes complicated in practice through the fact that in parturition itself the accompanying psychical phenomena of which we are not able directly to observe, in addition to the chief traumatic experience, there occur also pleasurable or, at least, relatively pleasurable moments, to which one presumably can regress.[1]

We would like just to emphasize the fact that melancholia differs in a remarkable way from the purely neurotic symptoms in that it uses not only the body (or the Ego) as a means of representing the primal state, but also shows the tendency to use objects in the outer world, as, for instance, darkened rooms, in the same sense. This tendency we can designate as a psychotic " characteristic." Thus the melancholic, by his withdrawal from the outer world, to a certain

[1] It seems predominantly to be a matter of the *normal* possibilities of regression, which in contradistinction to mania have been called merely " euphoric." For the designation of this state of affect, the term " anxiety-pleasure " (*Angstlust*), coined by Hattingberg, would be very useful.

extent regresses from his adjustment to the same, while, on the other hand, the psychotic delusions, the content of which so obviously strives to re-establish the primal state, have to replace the outer world, no longer compatible with the libido, by the best of all worlds—namely, the intrauterine existence. Wherever one turns to such a case history, especially from among the wide group of the so-called *dementia præcox*, one finds many representations of the birth phantasy, which are in the last resort reproductions of their own primeval history, whether expressed in direct language robbed only of its affect, or whether in symbolic expression, the importance of which has become easily intelligible in the light of psychoanalytic dream investigation.

The first useful steps taken towards the understanding of the " content of the psychoses " we owe to the Zurich School of Psychiatry, under the leadership of Jung and Bleuler, which very early recognized the supreme importance of the psychoanalytic discoveries and used them in Psychiatry.[1] After Freud, in 1894, had brought into prominence the defence mechanism as an explanation of certain hallu-

---

[1] See Jung's review of the relevant literature in the *Jahrbuch für Psychoanalytische und psychopathol. Forschungen*, Bd. ii., 1910, pp. 356-388, the corresponding literature of German and Austrian authors reviewed by Abraham (see also his work " Die psychosexuellen Differenzen der Hysterie und Dementia præcox," 1908) in *Jahrb.*, i., p. 546 ff.; continued in *Jahrb.*, vi., 1914, p. 343 ff., and finally in *Bericht über die Fortschritte der Psychoanalyse in den Jahren*, 1914-1919, Vienna and Leipzig, 1921, p. 158 f. Special mention should also be made of Jung's first works: *Uber die Psychologie der Dementia præcox*, Halle, 1907, and *Der Inhalt der Psychose*, Leipzig and Vienna, 1908. Further, the relevant basic works of Honegger, Itten, Maeder, Nelken, Spielrein, and others in the different volumes of the *Jahrbuch*. Finally, Bleuler's large volume, *Dementia præcox oder Gruppe der Schizophrenien*, 1911, which tends for the most part to be an application of Freud's ideas to *Dementia præcox*.

cinatory psychoses, and in 1896 could prove for the first time that " repression " was also a determining factor in cases of paranoia,[1] a complete decade elapsed before the Zürich clinic undertook the first psychiatrical advance in this field. Soon after this (1911) Freud brought forward his broadly outlined analysis of a case of paranoia (Schreber). This, by linking on to his previous work, and also by making use of the valuable results of the Zürich school, established for the first time an understanding of the psychical mechanism and the structural formation of psychoses. The " homosexual " attitude and the patient's defence against this feminine libido position showed itself to be the most important part of the mechanism, which also is again to be subordinated to the general tendency to overcome the birth trauma[2] in the sense of identification with the mother and the function of bearing (anal child). Through these investigations of Freud's, the theoretical understanding of the psychoses has been made possible for the first time, and a number of Freud's pupils have since devoted their work to the subject.[3] Into general psychiatry these revolutionary conceptions naturally penetrate very slowly, but more recently they seem to have exercised a decisive influence on the younger generation of psychiatrists.[4] In the

[1] " The Defence Neuro-Psychoses " and " Further Remarks on the Defence Neuro-Psychoses," Coll. Papers, vol. i.

[2] In the classical paranoia, behind the boisterous symptoms, the primal symptom of anxiety can easily be discovered (being persecuted), just as behind the protective construction of the phobias or the reaction barriers of the obsessional neurosis.

[3] Literature, Jahrbuch, vi., p. 345 ff.; Bericht, p. 158.

[4] See especially the interesting work of Paul Schilder (Vienna) in his comprehensive presentation Seele und Leben (Springersche Monographien, Berlin, 1923). The work, appearing almost at the same time, of Alfred Storch (Tübingen: The Primitive

foreground stands the phylogenetic point of view, which is an undisputed merit of the Zürich school (Honegger, Jung), but against the methodical misuse of which Freud already turned his attention when he showed how much there is still accessible and intelligible in the individual analysis, before one need turn to the phylogenetic material or view-point. Naturally this warning has not been of much use, and so we now see the advanced psychiatrists involved in a descriptive comparison of the psychology of the schizophrenic with that of the primitives.[1] When, for instance, in his interesting work, Storch compares the archaic-primitive attitude to the " magic-tabuistic " attitude and emphasizes the " mystical union " as well as the " cosmic identification," he retrogresses from Psychoanalysis in so far as he does not use the analytic understanding of the primitive attitude as an explanation of the schizophrenics; is content with a juxtaposition, without noticing that he has only replaced an obviously simple problem of individual psychology by a more complicated ethnological one.

Our concept tends rather to lead to a further understanding of individual psychology, and so also to find further explanations of the psychological enigma in ethnology. The viewpoint of the fundamental importance of the birth trauma, here represented, seems to us actually to facilitate the solution of this problem. The regressive tendency is so strongly pronounced in psychoses, that we may expect to find in them

---

Archaic Forms of Inner Experiences and Thought in Schizophrenia) rests almost entirely on the analytic conception without admitting this so unreservedly as Schilder. Purely analytic are the valuable contributions by Nunberg in the *Internat. Zschr. für Psychoanalyse.*

[1] See also Prinzhorn's work, interesting in its material, *Bildnerei der Geisteskranken*, Berlin, 1922.

the nearest approach to the primal situation. Actually the content of psychoses, whether obviously or in the patient's own symptoms of collapse of thought and speech, achieves complete representation, in the most extended form, of the intrauterine state and of birth.

We owe it to the industrious work of psychiatrists, that through the detailed communication of patients' case histories already valued from the psychoanalytic point of view, we are in the position to confirm in so striking a way the experiences gained from the analysis of neuroses. Having referred to the large amount of material relating to the psychoses in the literature already quoted, I would like to give some illustrations from Storch's last publication known to me. "A patient approaching a stuporous state makes continuous revolving motions with his hand round the navel. On being questioned he explains he wants to make a hole (what for?) in order to come out into freedom. Nothing further is to be learnt from him." It is, however, clear that the patient unconsciously means by it the return into the womb, otherwise the "symbol" remains unintelligible. Likewise for a manifestly expressed castration action there is the same motive; "the patient one day, after the above-mentioned incident, bit off a part of his finger; only after overcoming many inhibitions did he give a motive: 'In biting off part of my finger I have drawn the other people to me, in order to show that there is something missing in one place.' After further questioning, he continued: 'I wanted freedom; through the *hole* I have *crept out* like a *beetle*'" (p. 7). Storch assumes that this does not only mean leaving the clinic in the analytic sense, but also suggests the "vague" idea of freeing from the womb (birth through the navel), and remarks in addition, that to the patient as to so many schizophrenics, the idea of a re-embodiment was throughout a self-evident fact; just as re-incarnation was to primitive folk. A young schizophrenic, who as a child had been misused by her own father and ran away from service, experienced in a catatonic state a birth phantasy in which she appeared at the same time as the Christ child and his mother (p. 61). The same patient spoke of " a splitting of her own youth from her present person." She had the feeling that there *were two persons in her body*, one representing the ugly past and another who was in a high position beyond sex (pp. 77-78). Another patient (p. 63) made the nurse her " Lord God," and said " everything is comprehended in myself and the nurse, everything from Christ to the very lowest thing." (On being questioned about her relation to the nurse), " *We are completely one, both one ;* she is the Lord God, I am the same as she. I am in the nurse and the nurse is in me." Another time she said, " she has the whole world in herself," and explained this (on being questioned) in a characteristic way (p. 80).

Some patients show the regressive tendency in the form of a wish not to be grown up, the counterpart of which one often finds in children, as the longing to be grown-up. " A schizophrenic, in the thirties, complained in an excited tone, that he was turned into a child; I am no longer a man, but am already a child; when my wife visited me, I was not the husband belonging to the wife; I sat beside her as a child, by its mother " (p. 57). In contrast to other cases, where " the change into the feminine or childish state of life is experienced by the patients as a diminishing and depreciating of their Ego," Storch remarks, " we often meet with the opposite experience in young schizophrenics, who even step *over the threshold of childhood* into the life of a grown-up being; not seldom we find in them a pronounced fear of life and *of being grown up*, under circumstances in conflict with a strong desire to live and a need for love. From this conflict they want to flee back again into childhood . . ." (p. 89). I think that in this tendency we have before us the kernel which would justify psychologically the designation of this form of illness as dementia præcox. Others directly restore the old cloaca theory, that is, the abode in the womb, like the patient (p. 42) who "did not, indeed, believe that children are born through the rectum, but that between the ' pouch,' in which according to her opinion the child grows in the mother, and the lowest part of the bowel, there exists a passage through which the embryo can empty its dirt. The child is in the ' pouch ' and sucks inside at the little nipples giving nourishment (which are in place of the breasts). From the ' pouch ' an ' outlet ' goes to the rectum, ' so that the child is purged of the food which it takes with the milk.' Before parturition the outlet heals up, goes away, is for a cleansing purpose." Another catatonic with coprophagia explicitly gave the embryonal motivation for her act, when she stated " that during her psychotic conditions she was compelled to drink urine and to eat fæces "; after having previously lived through the sensation of dying, she meant that she needed the substance for her *building up* again. In a catatonic case analytically and thoroughly investigated by Nunberg, swallowing excrement signified self-fructifying and renewing.[1] Summing up, Storch says (in the chapter on " Rebirth "): " We meet with the idea of being dead and reawakened, the idea of going through to death, of becoming

[1] " Über den katatonischen Anfall," *Internat. Zschr. f. Psychoanalyse*, vi., 1921.

new and finally becoming god; we also find the *primitive sensual* expressions of rebirth, *the idea of really being born,* and so forth. Thus the complex thoughts of patients often rush pell-mell into the ideas of birth and pregnancy, *giving birth* and *being born, being the mother and the child "* (p. 76).[1]

Not only the content of the delusions seems clearly determined in this direction, but the psychotic states such as hallucinations, twilight and catatonic phases, also become intelligible as far-reaching regressions to the fœtal state. We owe the first bold attempt to formulate such a conception from analytic material to the valuable work of Tausk, who died prematurely. His paper is entitled " Über die Entstehung des Beeinflussungsapparates in der Schizophrenie,"[2] and he conceives this apparatus by which the patient thinks he is influenced as a projection of one's own genitalized body in the womb. " The projection of one's own body would thus be a defence against a libido position which corresponds to the development at the final stage of the fœtal condition and at the beginning of the extrauterine development " ·(*l.c.*, p. 23). From here onwards Tausk attempts to explain different schizophrenic symptoms. " Could not catalepsy, *flexibilitas cerea*, correspond to that stage in which the human being perceives his organs as not his own, and in which he must resign them, as not belonging to himself, to the force of a strange will ? Could not the catatonic stupor, which represents a complete rejection of the outer world, be a withdrawal into the womb ? Might not these extremely severe catatonic symptoms be the *ultimum refugium* of a psyche which also gives up the most

[1] Italics mine.
[2] *Internat. Zschr. f. Psychoanalyse*, v., 1919.

primitive Ego functioning and withdraws completely into the fœtal and suckling point of view. . . . The catatonic symptom, the negativistic rigidity of the schizophrenics, is nothing other than a renunciation of the outer world, expressed in 'organ speech.' Does not also the suckling-reflex movement in the final stage of progressive paralysis express such regression to the life of the suckling ? This regression to the suckling stage and even back as far as to the fœtal state— the last, indeed, only as a threat with a development of disease as its consequence—may become conscious to many patients. A patient said to me: ' I feel that I am getting younger and smaller all the time; now I am four years old, then I shall come to the swaddling clothes stage, and finally back into the mother ' " (p. 23 f.). Tausk therefore thinks that the phantasy of the return to the womb,[1] which must be accepted as a further atavistically performed " primal phantasy," comes up symptomatically " as a pathological reality in the regressive psyche of schizophrenics."

If at this point one introduces the reality of the birth trauma with its momentous after-effects, then not only can one affirm Tausk's assumptions, but one also comes to a really fundamental understanding of other psychotic symptoms, which relate directly to the birth trauma, and only indirectly to the intrauterine stage. This is true of all seizures and attacks, especially the so-called *epileptic*,[2] which in content and form betray the clearest reminiscences

---

[1] He remarks besides that the expression womb-phantasy (*Mutterleibphantasie*) originated from Gustav Grüner.

[2] In his work (likewise fundamental for the concept here brought to the fore) entitled " Stages in the Development of the Sense of Reality," *Contributions to Psycho-Analysis*, p. 181, Ferenczi has already alluded to the traceability of epileptic attacks to an early phase of language by gestures.

of parturition. There, moreover, we find a similar division as in circular insanity (cyclothymia), although without the reversal of the order in the latter. For the *aura* preceding the great epileptic attack, with its feeling of blessedness described so wonderfully by Dostoievski, corresponds to the pre-natal libido gratification, whilst the convulsions themselves reproduce the act of birth.

All these psychotic symptoms have in common the fact that they represent in the analytic sense a further regression of the libido than the neuroses. For, by freeing their libido from the outer world, replacing the mother, they supplement the loss of the primal object by a so-called cosmological projection, by which they only go back again to the primal situation through the incorporation (introjection) of objects with their Ego (mother and child). In this peculiar psychotic mechanism, which contains a disturbance of the relation to the outer world, the classical *paranoia*—and the paranoid forms of psychoses—stand closest to the mythological world view.[1] Paranoia seems characterized by the fact that in it the outer world is charged with libido far exceeding that in a normal adjustment; the whole world is, so to say, a womb, to the hostile influence of which the patient is now exposed (electric currents, etc.).[2] By means

[1] See the " paranoid " characterization in the mythical phantasy formation in *The Myth of the Birth of the Hero*.

[2] It is worthy of note that the paranoiac, Strindberg, has recognized in the pre-natal influence the explanation for the child's first reactions—namely, fear and hunger (in his autobiographical work: *Die Beichte eines Thoren*). To the references given there for providing for the pregnant, allusions only can be made. We may here reproduce some utterances of Strindberg's which are specially expressive in this connection (according to Storch, *l.c.*, p. 46 f.). When his loved one is taken by a stranger, it is for him " a *shock* to his whole psychic being," for " it was *a part of himself*, which *was taken*

of the reversal of feeling (hate) towards the father, the entire situation of the mother's protecting womb, in its cultural and cosmological significance, has here become a unique, gigantic, hostile entity, which pursues the hero, identified with the father, and ever challenges him to new battles.

In the meaning of this tendency to return to the mother, which the psychotic strives after by means of projection, the course of the psychotic disease, as Freud recognized, is actually to be interpreted as an attempt to cure. We see this clearly in the analytic process of healing, from which we started. Only the psychotic loses the way to the light of health in the underground labyrinth of the womb situation, whilst the neurotic is enabled to find the way to life again, by the Ariadne-like threads of remembrances thrown to him by the analyst.

---

by another, a part of his *bowels*, with which one now plays" (*A Soul's Development*, chap. 5). " In love, he melts together with the loved woman, but then when he has lost himself and his form, the desire for self-preservation grows, and in the anxiety at ' losing his Ego through the equalizing power of love' he attempts to free himself from her in order to find himself again *as self existing*" ("Entzweit," chaps. 2-3). After the psychosis he withdraws himself into loneliness, encloses himself " within the cocoon of his own soul " ("Einsam," chap. 3). From his later schizophrenic times he tells of protective measures which he uses against the currents disturbing at night; "When one is exposed to the *currents of a woman mostly during sleep*, one can isolate oneself "; " Incidentally one evening I placed a woollen *shawl over my shoulders and neck*, and this night I was protected although I noticed the attacks of currents." Finally, he shows also that the " idea of persecution " is linked on to anxiety in which he makes the " *panicky* frignt at everything and nothing " responsible for his restlessness. Strindberg's sad childhood and his peculiar " mother complex " are well known (see the allusion in *Inzestmotiv*, 1912, p. 32, note). From this point onwards, one can understand his whole development, personality, achievement, and psychosis.

As, according to the Freudian concept, hysteria is closely related to artistic production, the obsessional neurosis to the formation of religion and philosophic speculation, so the psychoses are closely related to the mythological world view. When analytically adjusted psychiatrists have recognized that the content of the psychosis is " cosmologic," we need not avoid the next step, that of analysis of cosmology itself, for then we shall find that it is nothing other than the infantile recollection of one's own birth projected on to Nature. As I am reserving the more detailed foundation of this concept in the rich soil of mythical and cosmological material for a book planned long ago under the title *Mikrokosmos und Makrokosmos*, I can here only refer to my various preliminary studies in the field of mythology, which attempt to show that the human problem of birth stands actually at the centre of mythical as of infantile interest and determines conclusively the content of phantasy formations.[1]

[1] See the works: *The Myth of the Birth of the Hero*, 1909; *Die Lohengrinsage* (1911); *Das Inzestmotiv in Dichtung und Sage* (1912), especially chap. ix., " Die Welternmythe "); and finally *Psychoanalytische Beiträge zur Mythenforschung*, collected studies in the year 1911-1914; second and altered edition, 1922 (especially " Die Sintflutsage," " Verschlingungsmythen," " Tiermärchen," etc.).

SYMBOLIC ADAPTATION

BEFORE turning to the mythical elaborations of the birth trauma exhibited in such impressive compensatory creations as hero formation, we must examine those facts which touch us more closely and are of more human consequence, showing as they do in an overwhelming manner the fundamental importance of the birth trauma and the everlasting longing to overcome it. These biological facts can also make intelligible to us the normal adjustment lying between asocial neurotics and exaggerated heroic accomplishment, and can explain, moreover, how this adjustment or adaptation, which we call culture and civilization, could succeed at all.

The condition of sleep, which takes place automatically every night, urges us to the idea that even the normal individual never completely overcomes the birth trauma, since he spends half his life in a state similar to that of the intrauterine.[1] We fall into this state automatically as soon as it is dark, thus again, as in the case of the child's fear of the dark room, when the external conditions urge the Unconscious to an identification with the primal state. Hence the approach of darkness is anthropomorphically conceived

---

[1] See especially Freud, *Introduction to Psychoanalysis*, and Ferenczi, " States in the Development of the Sense of Reality " (*l.c.*)

Neurotic *sleeplessness*, like somnambulism in all its forms, seems regularly to rest on a too intense repression of this biological necessity at the cost of libidinal strivings (to the mother). The frequent fear of being buried alive also falls in this category (Freud, *The Interpretation of Dreams*), just as its " perverted " counterpart, *necrophilia*.

74

in the imagination of all races as the return of the sun to the womb (underworld).[1]

In the state of sleep, in which we daily return to a considerable degree to the intrauterine situation, we dream, and there we make use of curious symbols which were known to the ancients, and which have been empirically established by Psychoanalysis, but are not yet completely understood in their origin and general human importance. Now dreams, from which we start in the analytical healing process (Chapter I.), show that these symbols, regularly appearing in *the wish dream*, ultimately represent the abode in the womb. On the other hand, in the *anxiety dream* the *birth trauma*, the expulsion from Paradise, is often reproduced with all its really experienced physical sensations and details. The hallucinatory wish fulfilment of the narcissistic dream-Ego, for the understanding of which Freud goes back to the

[1] The *moon*, with its *periodic* waxing and waning, seems to fit still better into the mythological representation of the constantly renewed longing to return, and appears in myths not only directly as a pregnant woman and one giving birth, but also as the disappearing and returning child. The goddess of the moon is also of importance as giving help in birth (midwife), which is connected with her influence on menstruation. The "congruence of a woman's menstruation and the lunar phases, which in our popular beliefs is still identical," leads Th. W. Danzel to think that the astronomic-cosmic period arose first into consciousness as a symbolic expression of *subjective periods* and rhythms, and is the foundation for the calendar which, in the astral countries (China, Babylon, Egypt, Mexico), was originally a " Book of good and evil Days " (see *Mexico*, vol. i., p. 28 [" Kulturen der Erde," vol. xi.], Darmstadt, 1922). " The period of 260 days of *tonal-anatl*, which plays a special rôle in the Mexican calendar, has perhaps as a foundation besides the astronomic periods also the *duration of pregnancy* (Danzel, *Mexico*, ii., p. 25, Darmstadt, 1922). Fuhrmann (*Mexico*, iii.) raises this assumption to greater certainty in tracing back the Mexican *year* to the pre-natal period of human beings, and the new (not based on the sun's course) time-reckoning to this *embryonal year* (p. 21).

embryonal condition,[1] is really proved by dreams completely uninfluenced analytically, to be an actual return and repro- duction of the intrauterine situation, as already physically realized to a certain extent in the purely physiological condition of sleep. Indeed, dream formation shows in various ways—at least, according to its unconscious tendency to fulfil wishes, postulated by Freud—that it is a more com- plete return *in uterum* than seems to be accomplished through the mere physiological fact of sleep.[2]   The infantile character of the dream goes much further back and has a much deeper basis than we hitherto would admit because, with our con- sciousness created for the perception of the outer world, we could not previously grasp the character of this deepest Unconscious.

As I am reserving for publication some valuable analytic material, I can here only allude to the fact that the *wish* and *anxiety dreams*, regarded by Freud as the two main types, fit in perfectly with the concept of going back to the primal situation or with its painful interruption through the birth trauma.[3]   Yet I would like to mention a third type of Freud's —namely, the punishment dream—in which the dreamer, mostly successful in life, later reinstates himself into a painful

[1] "Metapsychological Supplement to the Theory of Dreams," *Coll. Papers*, vol. iv.

[2] We also claim to be better able to understand why dream life under the influence of the analytic situation begins to flourish and to grow so luxuriantly, often in such an astonishing way.

[3] The *awakening*, especially from anxiety dreams, regularly repeats the process of birth, the coming into the world; this is the meaning of the so-called " threshold symbolism " (Silberer), which seems also mythologically to have but one meaning, the birth situation (see Roheim, " The Significance of Stepping Over," *Int J. of Ps.A.*, iii., 1922, in addition to the preceding work by Frau Sokolnicka).   Moreover, the threshold birth symptom is also ex- pressed in the frequent twitching of the legs on going to sleep.

situation, as it seems, for "punishment." This, as Freud has pointed out, besides being a "masochistic" tendency, is a wish to restore youth, and finally has in view the pleasurable return to the womb. This is typically the case in the so-called examination-dream, an almost universal anxiety dream experience of mankind, going back to the anxiety border of the examination passed at school. The preconscious thoughts of consolation expressed in the dream, namely, that also *at that time* it went off well, refer regularly in the deepest Unconscious to parturition. What remains to be explained is the intense feeling of guilt, which is regularly attached to the primal wish to return to the womb, and which is obviously connected with the affect of anxiety at birth in the sense that its complete reproduction must be avoided by means of this guilt feeling, just as *being stuck* in the examination-situation prevents a further return to the primal trauma.

The opposite to the punishment dream, namely, *the dream of indulgence*, although it may be apparently caused by such real necessities as hunger or other bodily needs, can be explained as an attempt to re-establish the intrauterine situation. For with the physiological sleep situation there returns the tendency to uninhibited gratification of all physical needs in the intrauterine form. Enuresis, which at the sexual stage is pollution, has the same meaning as incest. Just on that account incest dreams frequently occur with pollution, and, on the other hand, pollution dreams nearly always represent an unconcealed desire for incest. But even the wish for the indulgence of sleep (which Freud emphasizes as essential for dream formation in general) corresponds to the tendency to return to the intrauterine situation.

All dreams of *physical sensations*, even when caused by external stimuli[1]—as the indulgence dreams are caused by inner stimuli—allow an unconstrained return to the primal situation. For instance, the sensation of cold caused by the bedclothes slipping off is interpreted by the Unconscious as the first loss of the protecting covering and is compensated for by a dream-like withdrawal into a symbolized womb. Likewise *sensations of inhibition or flying*, which frequently alternate in the same dreamer, the former sensation frequently occurring in individuals who had a difficult birth (hindrance), is used by the Unconscious in fulfilling its wish not to come away from the mother. But the latter flying sensation, changing the violent birth trauma into an easy floating out, as suggested by the stork fable, reproduces deep down in the Unconscious the state of well-being, namely, that of floating in the primal fœtal condition (*cf.* the winged angels, the souls of the yet unborn, etc.). The corresponding anxiety situation seems to be reproduced in *dreams of falling*.

We notice here summarily that our previous remarks concerning sensations and types of dreams refer to quite general dream experiences, the typical character of which is explained by the universal human experience of birth.[2]

---

[1] New light is shed here on the so-called experimental dreams. The applied stimuli are interpreted in the meaning of the experienced primal situation (position of the limbs, etc.), all the more as they are chosen by the experimenter according to his own unconscious experiences; the putting of masks on the face, stimuli to the nose, tickling the soles of the feet, etc.

[2] This is also valid for the so-called *tooth dreams*, which Jung already recognized as birth dreams in the case of women (quoted in Freud's *Interpretation of Dreams*, as also the example there given by me). In the meaning of our concept as here set forth, the *tertium comparationis* is the typical painless falling out of teeth, which

But our remarks hold good also for the dreams recognized by analysis as typical in their *latent content*, of which I would like to mention here the so-called *birth dream* (dreams of birth). According to my experience this certainly represents the wish (or disinclination) to have one's own child, but only by means of the reproduction of one's own birth or intra-uterine situation (in water). The reversal of direction, which for birth (coming out) is represented by plunging into the water, is to be explained as the simultaneous production of the trauma (plunge) and the regressive tendency, which it strives to neglect. This necessity simultaneously to repre-sent both these regressive tendencies in the manifest dream content[1] is of paramount importance for the understanding of dreams. It not only explains the Freudian observation that the so-called " biographical dreams " are as a rule to be translated backwards (that is, they end according to one's desires, with the intrauterine condition); but it also makes it obvious that a far more extensive use must be made of the technique of reversal in the interpretation of dreams, by which the secondary meaning of the so-called progressive tendency is clearly palpable in its relation to the regressive tendency. The double level, which is best seen[2] in birth dreams, is mostly expressed by the appearance of two generations or by the repetition of situations (for example, the act of birth itself, as also in the hero myth) and clearly

---

compensates for the severity of the trauma (pain). The interpre-tations given hitherto (birth, fear of death, castration, masturbation, etc.), can easily be subordinated to this primary meaning.

[1] See Freud, " Metapsychological Supplement to the Theory of Dreams," *Coll. Papers*, vol. iv.

[2] See also my earlier treatise, " Die Symbolschichtung im Weck-traum," *Jahrb.*, iv., 1912.

shows how the identification with the mother (from the Œdipus complex) is used to represent simultaneously mother and child, the latter, indeed, by means of the reproduction of one's own birth.

These dreams are thus the best proof of the primal narcissistic tendency of the dream Unconscious, and show that it can do nothing else than portray the situation which gratifies the primal narcissism in the completest way.[1] And thus also Jung's interpretation at the so-called "subjective level," of which so much anagogic misuse has been made, finds a real basis, as do all ostensibly prospective tendencies of the dream which, when unmasked, are projections of the womb situation into the future.[2]

[1] To a quite primitive stage of development belongs the mode of representation on one's own body and from one's own material, as it is re-established, for example, in hysterical attacks (Ferenczi, *Gebärdensprache*); Freud first called attention thereto, by showing how the hysteric represents on himself also the action, for instance the embrace, desired from the love partner, " General Remarks on Hysterical Attacks," 1909, and " Hysterical Phantasies and their Relation to Bisexuality," 1908, *Coll. Papers*, vol. ii. One must add to this the interesting observations of Köhler in his *Mentality of Apes*, where he shows that apes express what they want by indicating it on their own bodies. Thus a chimpanzee expressed the embrace which her master should give her by putting her arms round her own body.

[2] The so-called telepathic dreams are analytically easy to solve as projections of the primal situation into the future. Likewise the whole of modern occultism, which rests on the ancient Indian symbolism of rebirth, can be understood completely from the primal trauma and its projected elaboration (astrology). For example, the occultists are right in assuming that memories of things in dreams go back to a *previous life* of the dreamer, and were then of importance, only they project the pre-existence further back than to the intrauterine existence.

On the other hand, the basic idea of telepathy corresponds to something projected into the future, perhaps to something already once experienced, anticipated, *déjà vu*, which likewise can have

Finally, we must mention, on account of its general interest, another typical form of anxiety dream, which well shows us how all the prospective tendencies interpreted into the dream show the effect of the primal repression of the birth trauma. This is the so-called " dream of travelling," the characteristic details of which may easily be understood from the primal trauma. Such details as not catching the train, packing and not being ready, losing one's luggage, etc., which in the dream are so painfully realized can be understood only when one interprets the departure as meaning *separation from the mother*, and the luggage (trunk, box) as a symbolic substitute for the womb, which as we know is replaced by all kinds of vehicles such as ships, automobiles, railway carriages, waggons, etc. The apparent death symbolism (Stekel)[1] contained therein is just as preconscious as are any prospective tendencies (journey of life). The Unconscious can think of separation, departure, and dying only in terms of the wish-fulfilling regression to the womb, because it knows and can portray no other wish tendency. The *reversal tendency*, by which every forward movement in the dream must be interpreted as only a regression, explains simultaneously a number of

---

no other reference than to the pre-natal existence (compare with this Dr. Szilagyi's interesting material published under the title " Der junge Spiritist," *Zschr.*, ix., 3, 1923. Quoted after the conclusion of this work.

[1] *The Language of Dreams*, 1922, where, in addition to Freud's dream investigation, a rich collection of the so-called " death symbolism " is brought together. Also in the chapter " Mutterleibsträume " there are a number of observations which, however, go beyond the merely practical " symbol interpretation " only with the supposition that perhaps a trace of memory may give the material basis for the birth dream.

otherwise unintelligible dream situations[1] (see the previous mention of the reversal of birth). It shows further that not the physical sensations alone (position, etc.), but also the apparently higher psychical functions (not only in dreams) of form, orientation and time[2] are related to the deepest of our unconscious wishes. The functional interpretation of single dream elements, which was certainly overestimated by Silberer and from which we have always inferred a " resistance " to the analytic interpretation, here manifests itself as a direct consequence of the tendency to flee away from the trauma. This tendency certainly

[1] The disinclination of so many people to sit with their back to the engine is thus explained. It is the same primal repression which forbids the mythical hero to look backwards on his way (turned into stone), which places the mocked-at hero the reverse way on the horse (Christ), and finds an echo in the manner of speech—" to put the cart before the horse." The childish *games of travel* (coachman, railway, etc.) show the corresponding pleasurable situation whereby in the meaning of the womb situation (waggon, ship, train, etc.) the absence of forward movement, which strikes adults as so laughable, forms just the exact wish-fulfilling element (see Peer Gynt's childish " journey " with the dying mother, after which his world's journey follows).

[2] In women who are analyzed during pregnancy and up till the time shortly before delivery, it is shown that time and especially numbers go back to pregnancy and birth (months, years, children, brothers and sisters, etc.), in which the birthday plays a quite special part, and on which most analyses of numbers rest. One ought not to wonder at there being in the unconscious, instead of the number 9, referring to the nine months of pregnancy according to the artificial sun calendar, other numbers corresponding to the " natural moon calendar " (see note 1, p. 75), as also in mythology the sacred numbers oscillate between 7, 9, 10. For instance, there are in Mexico 9 underworlds, in New Zealand 10 (" the lowest layer, *meto*, or place of decomposition, is where is completed the process of change of the decomposing corpse into the form of a worm," Danzel, *Mexiko*, i., p. 21). In China, the ten infernos are in the bowels of the earth, and are called " the prisons of earth," etc.

follows the established psychical channels, and in the psychical development of the individual probably leads from the repression of the primal trauma to the development of the so-called higher functions.

Before we turn from dream symbolism to a comprehensive understanding of symbols in general and their use in cultural adjustment to civilization, we should like specially to emphasize that our view of the paramount importance of the birth trauma finds its strongest support in the analytic interpretation of dreams. But a more detailed representation of this I must reserve for a bigger work. The fact must be stressed, however, that the previously mentioned analytic experiences enable us to give a real basis to the " womb phantasy," discovered long ago by Freud in analysis, and since corroborated by numerous examples in the literature of analysis. As the consequence of this experience seems of such great importance, there should be no doubt as to its meaning It is not to be denied that there is a *phantasy of going back* into the womb,[1] or that there is a wish tendency at a still later stage of development, illustrated by Silberer in excellent examples of " spermatozoa dreams," to go back into the father's body.[2] These are, as we said, phantasies which are partly connected with explanations about sex heard or read of at a later date. But in reality, as opposed to phantasy, in dream formation there occur during analysis many definite but quite unconscious reminiscences

[1] The classical presentation is to be found in a book written in 1795 under a pseudonym entitled *Meine Geschichte eh' ich geboren wurde. Eine anständige Posse vom Mann im grauen Rocke* (Neudrücke literarhistorischer Seltenheiten Nr. 2, Berlin, J. Ernst Frensdorff).

[2] Silberer, " Spermatozoenträume " and " Zur Frage der Spermatozoenträume," *Jahrb.*, iv., 1912).

or reproductions of the individual intrauterine posture, or peculiarities relating to one's own birth. These could arise from no conscious memory or phantasy formation, because they could not be known previously by anyone. The dream naturally uses subsequently what has been learnt from hearsay about one's own birth, but often in such characteristic ways that one is compelled to consider the dreamer's unconscious impression (often an impression in the literal sense of the word) as being right in preference to his conscious memory. That the period of dwelling in the father's body is able to be reproduced I would not care to maintain. On the contrary, it seems to me that if one continued the analysis of these " spermatozoa dreams " from the point of view here set forth, they would finally prove to be " back to the womb " dreams which have been remodelled by means of a later acquired conscious knowledge.[1] Often enough, indeed, the so-called " spermatozoa dreams " prove to be directly disguised " womb dreams," since the only way to come again to the mother's body is by way of the father's spermatozoa. Hence these dreams in no way conform to phantasies of returning to the father's body, but they are used rather as a means of newly *severing oneself* from the father in order to be permanently united to the mother. For the fœtal situation— at least, in the last period of pregnancy—and the birth situation itself are directly apprehended by the individual, and as such are certainly capable of being reproduced. We maintain, then, neither more nor less than *the reality of " the womb phantasy "* as it is manifested in child life, in neurotic symptoms, and in the physiological state of sleep (dream).

If we try to draw the most obvious conclusion from this fact, we must be prepared to meet various objec-

[1] Winterstein has rightly assumed this (*Imago*, ii., 1913, p. 219).

tions which will maintain that we are neglecting reality so called, namely the outer world, against which even the power of the Unconscious, no matter how great we think it, must ultimately find its natural limits. Naturally we do not want to go so far as to deny the external world, although the greatest thinkers in the history of the human mind, including Schopenhauer in his idealistic philosophy, approach such a conception. The "world as idea," that is, as my individual idea in my Ego, still has good psychological grounds, the analytic disclosure of which does not restrict the reality of the outer world and yet explains the force of the "Idea." If we divide everything opposed to the Ego in the outer world into objects of nature and everything else into objects created by man, then we have two groups which we can comprehend under the names Nature and Culture. Starting from the most primitive discoveries of culture such as fire and implements up to the most complicated technical machinery, it can be shown that these are not only made by man, but are also formed according to the image of man,[1] whose anthropomorphic world view thus gains support. It would lead us too far to give detailed reasons for this conception, which has the strongest support in the whole history of mankind as well as from the analytic point of view. What it is essential to understand is the psychological mechanism, by means of which every "discovery" is only a rediscovery of something latent, and the whole process of culture, as reflected in myths, is only a

---

[1] See Ferenczi's allusion to the "Psychogenese der Mechanik" (*Imago*, v., 1919), and the works quoted there of Mach, E. Kapp, and others. In addition, *Die Maschine in der Karikatur*, by H. Wettich (with 260 illustrations), Berlin, 1916, and *Die Technik im Lichte der Karikatur*, by Dr. Anton Klima (with 139 illustrations), Vienna, 1913.

human creation of the world on the pattern of one's own individual creation.

The study and understanding of so-called dream symbolism now enables us to trace back cultural creation to its origin in the depths of the Unconscious. From the overwhelming and confusing mass of existing cultural material, which humanity, compelled by the same old primal yearning, still constantly produces, we shall mention here only one example. This has already been brought to our attention for the understanding of infantile anxiety, and it places us in the midst of our sphere of culture, yet at the same time affords us a glance back to its historical development. It concerns the room, the space, which for the Unconscious regularly symbolizes the female genitals. And, indeed, ultimately it symbolizes the womb as relating to the only female genital known to the Unconscious, and the place in which before the birth trauma one was protected and warmed. There is now no doubt, according to anthropological investigations, that just as the coffin and its primitive forerunners the tree, the earth, the doubled-up burial position (embryonal posture), merely copy the womb situation, to which after death one wishes to return, so the primitive dwellings of the living, whether caves[1] or hollow trees,[2] were made or chosen

[1] Roheim gives American material for birth hollows in an article entitled " Primitive Man and Environment " (*Internat. Journal of Psychoanalysis*, ii., 1921, p. 170 ff. From the rich material quoted, that of W. Matthews, who has recognized the birth symbolism in the myths in question, is worthy of special notice (" Myths of Gestation and Parturition," *Americ. Anthropol.*, iv., 1902, p. 737).

[2] Emil Lorenz in a study " Der politische Mythus, Beiträge zur Mythologie der Kultur " (*Imago*, vi., 1920, and separately enlarged, 1922), linking on to Jung's mythological and Ferenczi's biological point of view, has emphatically shown this symbolic importance, and has proposed the term " psychic integral " for the understanding

in instinctive remembrance of the warm, protecting womb, analogous to the birds building nests for protective covering. Whatever has developed later in the course of continuous repression, which involves a gradual withdrawal from the primal trauma into sublimated forms substituting the primal state, is still quite obviously in the deepest sense linked to that primal situation. This we can see in the way in which the present-day child expresses fear when alone in a dark room. Whether it is the primitive hut covered with foliage (nest), or the "altar" which originates from the hearth fire (warmth from the mother), or the prototype of the temple (such as the Indian cave temple) which represented the roof or house as protection for this fire; whether it is the exaggerated Oriental temple buildings answering the purpose of the heavenly and cosmic projection of these human dwellings (tower of Babel), attaining the highest artistic idealization of their human origin in the Greek temple with its pillars replacing the primitive tree-trunks and representing human legs and with its variously formed capitals representing heads, as is naïvely allegorized in the Song of Songs; or whether it is the Gothic churches of the Middle Ages with their return to the upward reaching and yet depressing dark vaults; or finally, whether it is the American skyscraper with its flat, outer surface and the elevator shafts within; everywhere it is a matter of a reproduction, extending beyond the mere "symbol formation" of the dream or even of art, everywhere it is creative shaping of approved objects, approximating in form to the substitution of the primal situation.

---

of the adaptation of reality to our wishes and needs under the determining influence of the prototype of the first severance of the complete Ego from the world by means of the mother-image.

This simple case of "symbolic" adaptation to reality opens up new vistas in the understanding of the development of culture: from the nursery, which is only an extension of the kangaroo's pouch and the bird's nest beyond the swaddling clothes and cradle, to the house,[1] instinctively formed to imitate the womb, thence to the protecting town,[2] the fort,[3] and thence linking on to the earlier mythical construction (projection or introjection) of Nature (earth, cosmos), on the one hand, and on the other hand to the social displacement-and-substitute-formations of such concepts as fatherland, nation, and state. These latter, according to

[1] The *sacrifice to the building*, which consisted originally in walling up a living child into the foundation of a new house, should make clear the character of the building as womb substitute.

Ernst Fuhrmann, who in his interesting work has referred to the human physical prototype of secular and sacred buildings as the protecting room into which one creeps at night-time, or from which a new birth is expected (temple), refers also to a remarkable linguistic agreement, "The house corresponded to the skin (*Haus, Haut*), and to the water into which the sun goes, and also the entire group of words for *Dorf*, village, etc., shows that the idea of setting was connected with it. From *Haut* (skin) are derived *Hut* (hat), *Hütte* (huts), *Haus* (house); from *Fell* (pelt) were derived *Ville* (village), *Bull*. From *Schaf* (sheep), *Schuppen* (shed), also Russian *schuba*, *Pelz* (pelt). From *Wat* (water) were derived *bett, beth* (Hebrew), house, *Ved* in Swedish, *Wald* (wood), *Holz* (wood). When a man went to bed, he reached the water. The coverings between which he lay were the waves, and they were made of a material which was soft and flowing. On the posts of the bed were frequently carvings which had reference to the monsters of the underworld, but also angels, the spirits who brought the body to life again had to be present . . ." (*Der Sinn im Gegenstand*, München, 1923; and *Der Grabbau*, Munich, 1923, 43 and ff.).

[2] For the town as mother symbol, *cf.* my work *Um Städte werben*, 1911. The seven hills of Rome correspond to the teats of the she-wolf.

[3] *Burg* (fort) from *Berg* (mountain), *verbergen* (to hide), originally *Fluchtburg* (refuge), (Lorenz, p. 87).

Freud's reconstruction,[1] link on to the history of the primal horde, and to the common possession and renunciation of the primitive mother in the later social community.

As Freud has shown, the primal father is slain by the sons who succeed in possessing the mother, or in other words, wanted to return to the mother. This was prevented in the primal horde by the " strongest male," the " father," who was the external opponent and object of " fear " (of the mother). But the reason for renunciation is—as the primitive orgiastic death feasts show—that although all take possession of the mother sexually (promiscuity), not all can return into her. This is the real psychical motive for the " heroic lie," namely, the fact that in the myths and fairy tales there is only one who is able to do the primal deed with the mother, and he is the youngest, who has no successor.

From this psychological motive there follows the formation of man-governed states, so momentous for human development, since it has now become socially necessary for a single individual to take the father's place by identification with him, thus breaking through the ban on the inaccessible mother which finds its sociological expression in the so-called " Mother Right."[2] The establishment of the father's power thus follows, whilst the fear of the mother, moderated into respect, is transferred to the new usurper of the father's place, namely, the captain, leader, king, etc. The protection afforded him by reason of certain privileges or contracts against a repetition of the primitive crime, namely, being slain, he owes to the fact that he has taken the mother's place, and so by

---

[1] *Totem and Taboo. Group Psychology and the Analysis of the Ego*, 1921.

[2] Bachofen, *Das Mutterrecht*, 1861 (second unchanged edition, 1897).

a partial identification with the mother he takes over the privileges belonging to her. In the so-called dominance of the Father Right, right or justice—*i.e.*, the privilege of mutual (conciliatory) protection, social forbearance, and care of others—springs from the natural phase of mother attachment which, on the one hand, rests on the protection given by the mother (womb), on the other hand is due to the fear of her caused ultimately by the birth trauma. The peculiar ambivalence towards the lord, the ruler, is thus explained. He is loved, protected, and spared, that is taboo,[1] in so far as he represents the mother. He is hated, tortured, or slain, as representative of the primitive enemy near the mother. In all the restrictions or ceremonials imposed on him, which often seem completely to cancel his " rights," he himself partially returns into the pleasurable primal situation, to the place where even the King must go unaccompanied and on foot.

This is especially clear in the " cult of the sun," the significance of which is by no means exhausted in the conscious identification with the powerful father. On the contrary, it has its deeper-lying unconscious sources of pleasure in the original idea of birth, according to which the daily rising and setting of the sun is conceived of as the new-born child returning at night time to the mother (sun—son). This is clearly expressed in the life of the Peruvian rulers, whose ceremonial conforms to identification with the sun. The " Inca " never goes on foot, but is always carried in a sedan chair. He does not feed himself, but is fed by his wives. He wears a robe only for one day, then lays it aside, and after six months this robe is taken away and burnt. The Inca

---

[1] The primal taboo is the maternal genital which from the beginning onwards is invested with ambivalent feeling (holy-cursed).

takes food only once out of the same dish, everything he uses only once. . . . Thus the Inca becomes every day a new being, he is the women's suckling who has to be fed by them.[1] The Inca is an entirely ephemeral being in *statu nascendi*, so Fuhrmann rightly sums up the situation. But every ruler must submit more or less to a similar ceremonial of birth. The Priest-King of New Guinea may not move, and must even sleep in a sitting posture (in order to provide equable atmospheric conditions). In Japan's olden days the Mikado had to sit on the throne every forenoon for some hours at a time with the crown on his head (today our children's idea of " ruling " really means to exercise omnipotence on earth); but he must remain stiff as a statue, without moving hands or feet, head or eyes, otherwise evil will fall over the land (according to Kämpfer, *History of Japan*).[2]

The king therefore originally is not " father," but *son*, and indeed a little son, *infans*, a minor, " his majesty the child," who rules through the clemency of the mother.[3] We have already suggested how these earliest steps to a

[1] Fuhrmann, *Reich der Inka*, Hagen, 1922, p. 32 (*Kulturen der Erde*, vol. i.).

[2] But the king or god does not sit " like a statue," rather the statue perpetuates this blessed state of immobility (see chapter on art). The *crown*, the noblest of all head coverings, goes back originally to the embryonal caul, as also our hat today, the loss of which in a dream signifies separation from a part of one's Ego. *The sceptre*, of which there is no doubt as to its phallic signification, originates from the most primitive phase of the mother's dominance (woman with a penis), and thus the sceptre has for the male ruler originally the one meaning of making him again a man by this substitute—for the ruler was formerly castrated like the ancient priests, that is, was the mother (see the wooden copy which Isis has made of the lost phallus of Osiris. Rank, *Die Matrone von Ephesus*, 1913).

[3] Perhaps Kaiser, Cæsar, is connected with " to cut "; the one cut out (*cf.* also " Cæsarian " operation, *Kaiserschnitt* ?).

social organization, to the state in " children's shoes," may
have been taken.   The earlier high valuation of woman (her
genital), which is still apparent in the ancient worship of
goddesses and which has left its traces in the later " Mother
Right," had to be replaced by the social father-organiza-
tion traced by Freud from the primitive horde.   The strict,
just, but no longer violent father must again be set up as
the " barrier to incest " against the desire to return to the
mother, whereby he only assumes once more his original
biological function, namely, to sever the sons from the mother.
Anxiety of the mother is then transferred as respect to the
King, and to the inhibiting Ego (ideal) motives which he
represents (justice, state, etc.).   The sons' (burghers and
subjects) attitude towards him is that of the well-known two-
sided Œdipus libido.   The systematic social depreciation
of woman from her original heights finally results in a reaction against that infantile dependence on her, which the
son, now become father, can no longer bear.[1]

This is why the ultimate aim of every powerful and successful conqueror is to gain sole possession of the mother[2] (father
identification).   And every revolution which strives for the

[1] An extremely instructive illustration to this biological root of
" matriarchy " is that published by Leo Frobenius (*Das unbekannte
Afrika*, Munich, 1923, p. 23), and on p. 41 ff., illustrating this
meaning, is a drawing on rock from Tiot in Algeria, which shows a
hunter *bound by the navel string to the (praying) mother.*

[2] See L. Jekels " Der Wendepunkt im Leben Napoleons I," *Imago*,
iii., 1914, and William Boven, " Alexander der Grosse," *Imago*, viii.,
1922.

One must pay attention, moreover, to the characteristic confession of the young Napoleon who, on October 26, 1798, writes:
" There is seldom, perhaps, a more faint-hearted man than me.
When engaged on a military plan, *I am like a girl waiting for her
confinement.*   But if I have made my decision, then everything is
forgotten except that which will contribute to success."

overthrow of the masculine dominance shows the tendency to return to the mother. But these bloody revolutions against the dominance of the father are ultimately caused and made possible by woman, and that entirely in the sense of the mythical " heroic lie." As shown by the French revolution, it is less the king than the dissolute queen— characteristically suspected of committing incest with her son—the dominance of mistresses and of women in general, which stirred the rage of the crowd, and which also determines the predominating part of women in revolutionary movements.[1] Through her sexual power woman is dangerous to the community, the social structure of which rests on the fear displaced to the father. The king is slain by the people, not in order that they may be free, but that they may take upon themselves a heavier yoke, one that will protect them more surely from the mother:[2] *Le roi est mort, vive le roi*.[3]

Woman has an antisocial influence,[4] which gives psycho-

[1] See Beate Rank, " Zur Rolle der Frau in der Entwicklung der menschlichen Gesellschaft " (Lecture given at the Vienna Psychoanalytic Association, May, 1923).

[2] Bachofen (p. 31) derives *parricidium* of the Roman law, which originally signifies murder of the king or father, from *pareo*—to bear. " In the word parricidium, the act of birth is especially emphasized. Parricidium is the outrage committed on the primal mother in any of her offspring " (see also A. J. Storfer, *Zur Sonderstellung des Vatermordes. Eine rechtsgeschichtliche und völkerpsychologische Studie*, 1911).

[3] See also Paul Federn, *Die Vaterlosegesellschaft. Zur Psychologie der Revolution*, 1919, who comes to the conclusion that man cannot put up with a fatherless society for any length of time.

[4] Napoleon Buonaparte, when a lieutenant, wrote a dialogue on love, in which he says: " I maintain that *Love is harmful to society*, to the happiness of the individual; I think that it causes more evil than good, and I should consider it a benefit if the deity would free the world from it."

logical reasons for her exclusion from social as from political life in primitive (club houses) and in highly developed civilizations.[1] Man depreciates her only consciously; in the Unconscious he fears her. On this account she is also desexualized and idealized in the French Revolution as Goddess of Reason. And in ancient Greece, Athene was represented as born from the head of Zeus. "Freedom" (la Liberté) has always had a feminine form, and goes back finally to the freeing from the maternal prison (the storming of the Bastille).

The development of the paternal domination into an increasingly powerful state system administered by men is thus a continuance of the primal repression,[2] which has as its purpose the ever wider exclusion of woman—just on account of the painful memory of the birth trauma—even at the cost of establishing the uncertain descent (*semper incertus*) from the father as a foundation for the entire law (name, inheritance, etc.).[3] The same tendency completely to

[1] In his valuable work on "Die Pubertätsriten der Wilden," Th. Reik has shown how becoming a man is represented by a symbolic repetition of birth, namely by a detaching from the mother (*Imago*, iv., 1915-16).

[2] Winterstein, in addition to Bachofen, has already used this for the understanding of the formation of philosophical systems (*Imago*, ii., 1913, pp. 194 and 208).

[3] The original oath sworn by the testicles of the father (testes) on which our oath still rests (position of the fingers), is for the Unconscious always a false oath, since it knows the origin from the mother only, as the popular oaths and curses sufficiently prove, which all clearly and coarsely indicate the mother's body.

That the name "right," derived from the side of the body which physiologically is less concerned with the birth trauma and so is stronger, shows in what way these biological facts determine the development of mankind. The left, which appears so frequently in birth dreams as the endangered side, and which Bachofen has recognized in mythical traditions as the "maternal," was,

exclude the painful share of woman in one's own origin is preserved in all myths in which man creates the first woman, as, for example, in the biblical story of creation.

It seems, moreover, that a number of *discoveries* have as their aim the permanent establishment of the father's power, just as the previously mentioned creations of civilization aim at the permanent extension of the mother's protection. We mean the discovery of *implements* and *weapons*, all of which really directly imitate the masculine sexual organ, which in the biological development preceding any civilization was qualified to force its way into the yielding feminine material (mother).[1] As this can only be achieved to a degree that fails to satisfy the Unconscious, the attempt carried out upon this substitute material (*materia*) is brought to greater and greater perfection by means of implements which, as is well known, may be considered as improvements on other natural tools such as hands, feet, teeth, etc. But this task obtains its unconscious incentive from the mother libido, namely, the perpetual insatiable tendency to force one's way completely into the mother. In agreement with

---

owing to the anatomical peculiarities of human beings, ontogenetically destined to be considered inferior (the normal birth is in the left position). So also the (ethical) symbolism of right and left (meaning bad) to which Stekel has alluded, is rooted in the birth trauma—indeed, in the intrauterine state. See also the psychical peculiarities of the left-handed (Fliess and others), as well as Ferenczi's explanation of hysterical hemi-anæsthesia, " Erklärungsversuch einiger hysterischer Stigmata " (*Hysterie und Pathoneurosen*, 1919). In addition, there is, in Jewish mysticism, the concept that the left (feminine) repels, the right (masculine) attracts, also similar concepts in Chinese mysticism (Langer, *Die Erotik der Kabbala*, Prague, 1923, p. 125).

[1] Fritz Giese, " Sexualvorbilder bei einfachen Erfindungen," *Imago*, iii., 1914.

this is the surprising fact that the penis itself has, in consequence of the primal fear, experienced no similar artificial " lengthening " such as is represented by the tools for the other limbs,[1] and on to which even this tendency seems to be displaced, just as the mother is replaced by the *materia*. In this unwillingly achieved substitute (earth),[2] which is the first task of cultural adaptation, there now appears to have taken place a decisive and purely physical turning away from woman as the primal object of aggressive libido. It would seem that in *man's upright position*, in his *being raised from the earth*, which has recently been connected[3] with the invention of tools, we can see the decisive step in the process of actually becoming man, that is, in the cultural overcoming of the birth trauma by turning aside from the female genitals to an adjustment to the genitalized external world, which again ultimately has only a maternal signification.

Weapons in their origin were closely connected with tools or implements. It may be assumed that originally they were even identical and were used at the same time for the elaboration of material, as for the hunt (killing). The hunt itself again links on directly to the substitution for the

[1] In contrast to the enhancement of pleasure in the sexual act itself, as the customs (quoted p. 41, footnote 2) of the primitive peoples show, and which we may consider psychologically as a " preservative " from the fear of being completely engulfed.

[2] According to the (hitherto unpublished) bio-analytical investigations of Ferenczi, the earth itself seems to be a substitute for the primal mother of all living beings, the sea water (Meer als Muttersymbol).

[3] Paul Alsberg, *Das Menscheitsrätsel*. Versuch einer prinzipiellen Lösung (1922), who tries to represent the completion of man the other way round, as a result of the use of implements, and, indeed, originally as a result of throwing stones with the hands.

mother's nourishment, and indeed all the more directly, the further we go back. The warm blood of slain animals was drunk in direct continuance of the intrauterine nourishment, and the raw flesh was swallowed—lingering echoes of which still reach us in the myths of swallowing, where the hero in the interior of the animal eats of its soft parts. The "incorporation" of the animal's flesh, to the maternal significance of which Roheim has recently alluded,[1] is to be interpreted even at the stage of the totemistic father-sacrifice, in the sense of the intrauterine situation as a gift of the devoured creature's strength; just as the lion's skin in which Heracles covered himself lent him not merely the strength of the male animal (father), but also the invulnerability of the child protected *in utero* (compare with this the African hunting under the " protection " of the navel string). But here we must remind ourselves that, after all, every protection from elemental dangers or human attacks (with weapons), whether it be the hole in the earth or hollow trees, the mobile shield or war chariot, submarine or tank, ultimately signifies a flight to the mother's protective covering.[2] The warm hide (skin), which was likewise man's first protective covering against the cold, is thus the real counterpart to the mythical creeping into the animal's warm body.[3] Part of the ambi-

[1] " Nach dem Tode des Urvaters." Lecture given at the Congress in Berlin, September, 1922, *Imago*, ix., 1, 1923.

[2] This is shown in the classical tradition, according to which the Persian women checked the panic-stricken flight of their husbands and sons from the Medes, by uncovering their shame; *rogantes num in uteros matrium vel uxorum velint refugere* (Plutarch, *De virt. mulierum*, 5).

[3] The enveloping of the body in the warm skin of the newly slain animal holds good today among the people as a curative means because it establishes the pre-natal situation.

The amnion, surrounding the embryo, was known to Empedocles

valence of the later sacrifices of animals, which already lies in the word "sacrifice," is explained from this maternal libidinal signification and is expressed in the regret that the partial realization of this primal situation is bound up with the killing of the mother (sadism). For the slaying of the mother there is substituted later the imposing totemistic sacrificial death of the primal father, entirely in the sense of the earlier mentioned substitution of the maternal libido object by the paternal Ego ideal.

This transition period is shown very beautifully in the great Mexican festival of the spring (*Ochpaniztli*—to sweep away), in which a woman representing the goddess *Tlazolteotl* was slain by cutting off her head. " Then was the *skin stripped from the sacrifice. With this skin a priest covered himself, and thenceforth represented the goddess in the further ceremonies.* From the thigh skin of the sacrifice a mask was made (*schenkelmaske*) with which the son of the goddess, the god of Maize, *Cintcotl*, was clothed " (Danzel, *Mexiko*, i., p. 43). These strange customs also represent a birth (that of the maize god) which is symbolized on the images of the goddess by the *sprawling attitude of the legs* (which seems to be connected with the thigh mask drawn over the son's head). It is obvious, moreover, that the transition from the sacrifice of the mother (the goddess) to the sacrifice of the father (the priest) proceeds by way of the son, who *in the course of this sacrifice enters again into the mother*. For the

---

by the name of " sheep skin " (see Schultz, *Dokumente der Gnosis*, 1910, pp. 22 and 128).

Thus clothes made from animal material, still predominant today, prove to be a simultaneous bodily protection from the cold (which one first experienced at birth), and libidinal gratification through a partial return into the mother's warm body.

original human sacrifice, as preserved in its purest form in the Mexican cult, leaves no doubt as to the fact that the victim sacrificed was identical with the one sent back into the mother, and that the sacrificial act itself was performed in order to cancel the process of birth.[1] " The thought of the captive sacrifice so dominated the views of the Mexicans that even the birth of a child was compared with the capturing of a prisoner. The woman who has borne a child is the warrior who has made a prisoner, and the woman who dies in childbirth is the warrior who has fallen into the hands of an enemy and is killed on the sacrificial stone " (Danzel, *Mexiko*, i., p. 29).[2] Accordingly, we find in the feast *Toxcatl* a boy victim, who has been worshipped for a year as the god and as whose representative he must be sacrificed. This year conforms to the previously mentioned embryonal period of 260 days, during which time the boy is constantly surrounded by *eight* pages, a girl being added (as ninth companion) for the last twenty days, (see Fuhrmann, *Mexiko*, iii., p. 15).

We believe we have understood " symbolism " as the most important means for adjustment to reality, in the sense that every " comfort " that civilization and technical knowledge continually strive to increase only tries to replace by durable substitutes the primal goal from which, in the meaning of so-called development, it becomes ever further removed. From this fact the peculiar character of the symbol is explained and the just as peculiar reactions to it of

---

[1] In the Mexican picture script the victim is mostly represented as a collapsing figure *with drawn-in limbs and head downwards* (Danzel, *Mexiko*, vol. i.).

[2] This conception is psychoanalytically explained by Alice Balint, " Die mexikanische Kriegshieroglyphe *atltlachinolli* " (*Imago*, ix., 4, 1923).

human beings, who easily recognize it in certain connections but in other connections turn away from it in indignation. For the real world itself, created by man, has proved to be a chain of symbol formations, uninterruptedly renewed, which must represent not merely a substitute for the lost primal reality which they copy as faithfully as possible, but at the same time must remind us as little as possible of the primal trauma connected with it.   This explains among other things how a modern invention, for example, the " Zeppelin," can be used as an *unconscious* symbol; because it is itself modelled upon the unconscious prototype which recognizes therein only itself.   And so in all practical discoveries it is ultimately only a matter of a reduction of external resistances to a productive libido gratification, approaching as closely as possible to the primal condition.   This is shown from the analysis of the mania to invent, which Kielholz has attempted in an interesting work.[1]   In some of his cases it is obvious that the patient who wishes to discover *perpetuum mobile* or the squaring of the circle wants in this way to solve the problem of permanently dwelling in and fitting into the mother's womb.   In other cases of electrical inventions (apparatus through which run warm unseen currents), etc., a detailed study of the patients' delusions ought to show clearly their importance as a reaction to the birth trauma.[2]

We have thus recognized " symbol formation " as the essentially *human* primal phenomenon which enables human beings to become different from animals, and instead of

[1] "Zur Genese und Dynamik des Erfinderwahns." A lecture given at the Berlin Congress, 1922.

[2] See Tausk's conjecture that the " electric currents " of the schizophrenics perhaps represent the sensation of the first nerve and muscle functioning of the new-born (*l.c.*, p. 28, note).

changing their own body (autoplastic),[1] as in the case of the giraffe, which stretches itself " to the covering "—that is, to the food—to change or mould the external world in the same way into an exact copy of the Unconscious (alloplastic). Yet there still remains for our consideration the intellectual means of expression which, along with the upright position of man, fundamentally separates him from the animals. I mean, of course, *speech* and its development. The remarkable discovery of analysis, that, on the one hand, in symbolism as a soundless universal language[2] we have resemblances that extend far beyond the boundaries of speech, and, on the other hand, that bewildering linguistic assonances and similar sounds are to be found among peoples in whom a direct influence seems excluded—this discovery becomes intelligible as soon as we understand " symbolism " not as a sediment of speech formation, and the formation of speech as a continuous development of the " primal symbolism." The dreams of animals which pass through a foetal development may be assumed to reproduce the situation in the womb, only they lack the means for linguistic expression so characteristic of human beings. Just how man has attained this is naturally connected with the phylogenetic development of the higher centres and functions. But over certain portions of individual development the origin and function of animal sounds are closely parallel to the primal stage

[1] According to Ferenczi, " Hysterische Materialisationsphänomene " (*Hysterie und Pathoneurosen*, 1919, p. 24); furthermore "that there appears in hysteria a part of the organic foundation on which symbolism in the psychical is built up," p. 29.

[2] Even Schelling emphasized in a work of his youth that the " oldest language of the world knew nothing else than sensuous indications of concepts." See also the work of Hans Apfelbach, *Das Denkgefühl. Eine Untersuchung über den emotionellen Charakter der Denkprozesse*, Wien, 1922.

of articulated speech. The first reaction after birth is the cry which, by violently abolishing the difficulty of breathing, may presumably relieve a certain amount of anxiety.[1] The same cry is then repeated as a desire for the mother, whence the formation of the lips, practised by the infant at the breast, leads as a wish motive to the formation of the universal human syllable *ma*.[2] This enables us to grasp the formation of sound from symbol *in statu nascendi*;[3] for the lips formed for sucking represent the first substitution of the mother by a, so to say, autoplastic attempt. Should the desire which causes the sucking formation of the lips be ungratified, then again is released the first painful cry of anxiety which signalized the separation from the mother. This conception also fits in with the theory of the sexual alluring call, which only repeats on the sexual level the desire for reunion with the object. Naturally also in word and speech formation, which is constantly becoming sexualized, in its later stages a good part of the primal symbolism proves to be surviving and at work.[4] Similarly in the next stage of substitution for words, namely, in writing and its previous stage of drawing (picture writing), a great part is still played by symbolism, which the artist then knows how to use for the purposes

[1] From the forced cry, a direct way leads according to Pfeifer's phylogenetic theory to voice formation and to song (Congress Lecture, Berlin, September, 1922). According to analytic conclusions the way to music seems to branch directly not from the birth trauma but from the intrauterine situation.

[2] See also S. Spielrein, " Die Entstehung der kindlichen Worte Papa und Mama," *Imago*, viii., 1922.

[3] The American school of Behavorists say that words were first formed plastically in the larynx.

[4] See Hans Sperber, " Über den Einfluss sexueller Momente auf Entstehung und Entwicklung der Sprache," *Imago*, i., 1912; and Berny, " Zur Hypothese des sexuellen Ursprungs der Sprache," *Imago*, ii., 1913.

of æsthetic enjoyment by rediscovering it and reproducing it in his own special way. Whilst the painful anxiety effects seen in the analyses of disturbances in speech (stuttering—stammering), as well as in the neologisms and in the speech distortions of the mentally diseased, again regress to the original symbol signification.[1]

We have thus surveyed the whole circle of human creation, from the nocturnal wish-dream to the adjustment to reality, as an attempt to materialize the primal situation—*i.e.*, to undo the primal trauma. From this survey the so-called advance in the development of civilization has proved to be a continually repeated attempt to adjust to the enforced removal from the mother the instinctive tendency to return to her. Following along the path of the development of culture, we will now trace the unmistakable approach to the primal trauma in the expression " Back to Nature !" But if we look more closely into the relation of man to Nature we recognize in it only a clearer kind of anthropomorphic assimilation which results in the apperception of everything cosmic in the same unconscious meaning that culture tries to reproduce. In mythology we see the most sublime survival of what is perhaps the most primitive adjustment both in the phylogenetic and also in the ontogenetic sense. For the new-born child could not live at all unless that part of the external world lying nearest to it and, finally, the world itself, were immediately made into a substitute for the mother; whether it be the hands of the midwife, or the warm water, or later the swaddling clothes, the bed, the room, etc. The phylogenetic counterpart is shown in myths where at first the tangible earth, and later the

[1] *Cf.* Freud, " The Unconscious," 1915, *Coll. Papers*, vol. iv., p. 129 ff.

heavens just on account of their unattainableness, appear as the protecting mother covering. Before the earth, by assimilation to the intrauterine life, water represented the maternal primal source, whilst this significance is given also to the sun as source of warmth and continues still to exist in the "symbolism" of fire. The mountains with their hollows and caves, with their forests (hair), were looked upon as a gigantic primal mother, stressing especially the protective characteristic. With the advancing knowledge of the inadequacy of all these given substitutes, we come to an actual creation of possibly more adequate culture formations, and in so far as these, too, are insufficient, we have the naïve parallel compensatory fantasy—formations of Paradise and a future life, as realistic Utopias or as idealistic lands of desire.

With regard, then, to the creations of man—*i.e.*, civilization in the narrowest and widest sense—we have to deal with adjustments to reality and supplementary phantasies which extend from the biologically-instinctive to the socially conscious acts, and which, from the point of view of *the adjustment of reality to the Unconscious, may be considered as the real principle of the development of man.*[1] With regard to the absorption of Nature into this "symbol-circle" given by the long period of the human fœtal stage, we have to deal with the mechanism of mythical projection by means of which man alone is in the position to subsume given "Nature" under these inborn primal forms. In this light we can explain the myths of world-creation and of "world-parents," which, in the process of cosmic assimilation,

[1] Brun shows biological first stages to this in the animal kingdom ("Selektionstheorie und Lustprinzip," *Internat. Zschr. f. Ps.A.*, ix., 2, 1923). Preliminary statements by Ferenczi, "Hysterische Materialisationsphänomene," 1919, p. 31.

have preserved for us the most sublime attempts to " undo " the birth trauma, to deny the separation from the mother.[1] The first conscious recognition of this severance was reserved for the philosophical theory of cognition with its distinction between the Ego and the non-Ego, after philosophic speculation had exhausted itself on the problem of "identity," which in the last resort lies hidden in the physiological relation of mother and child.

[1] Similarly the phantasies and myths of the end of the world (Schreber) which attain in the most radical "separation" the innermost reunion (absorption into the All). *The Flood* which initiates a new world period is nothing but a "universal" reaction to the birth trauma, as the myths of the origin of the earth or the sea also show. Moreover, here seems to lie the key to the understanding of the traditions of a new world period. This I will deal with elsewhere.

HEROIC COMPENSATION

WHEN we look back from our newly gained standpoint to the psychoanalytic investigation of myths, we notice that it was here, where the material speaks a more universal language than in the neuroses and psychoses, that the importance of the birth trauma was first brought home to us. Already "The Myth of the Birth of the Hero," which Freud with his keen observation had recognized as the nucleus of the myth formation, could have thrown full light on the question if we had been sharers in those analytic experiences, for they would have encouraged us to admit a still greater value in these "fairy tales" and, according to Freud's injunction,[1] to re-translate these phenomena of projection into psychology. Instead of this the general human tendency, to react with repression to any too clear approach to the recognition of the primal trauma, led to an evaporation of this first clear insight into Jung's anagogic ethical interpretation of myths.

The myth of the hero's birth begins, as is well known, with the situation of the child in the protecting womb (small box), where it is already persecuted by the father, who—in the meaning of the primal wish fulfilment—does not want the child to come into the world at all. The rest of the hero's fate is nothing but the working out of this situation, namely, the reaction to a specially severe birth trauma, which has to be mastered by over-compensatory achievements, among which the most prominent is the regaining of the mother.

[1] See *The Psychopathology of Everyday Life* (last chapter).

For these achievements, known as the deeds of a hero, are used in the myth exactly as in the neurosis and all other creations of the Unconscious for the purpose of winning again the primal situation in the mother, with the consequence that the father is fought as the chief object of resistance. As we recognized in the neurotic a human being who cannot, without harm, overcome the primal affect of anxiety arising in the birth trauma, so the hero represents the type who, being free from anxiety, seeks to overcome an apparently specially severe birth trauma by a compensatory repetition of it in his deeds. And so in the subsequently formed (infantile) wish phantasies, the hero is regularly one cut out of the mother's womb, and spared in this way from the beginning the trauma of anxiety. On the other hand, this theme of the myth of the hero's birth shows how difficult it has been at the beginning for the hero to leave the protecting womb to which behind the mask of such bold deeds of reform and conquest he constantly strives to return again. The theme of heroic *invulnerability* is also to be explained as a kind of permanent uterus, which the hero brings with him into the world as armour, horny skin or helmet (magic hood),[1] but which still betrays in the single mortal place, as, for example, Achilles' heel, how strongly even the hero was once purely physically attached to the mother.[2] On that account the motive of exposure, which

[1] Here also belong the " clouds " or " mist " of Athene, protecting the Trojan heroes in danger. Sometimes the hero is born in full armour, as Uitzilopochtli, the tribal hero of the Aztecs.

[2] In contrast to the " protected " head (caul, crown), which first leaves the womb, the feet, which come out last of all, are mostly the weak part. The swollen feet of Œdipus, besides Achilles' heel, show that it is a question of that part of the body which actually on leaving last touched the mother's genitals. This would also explain

simultaneously represents the return to the mother and the trauma of birth (plunging in), attempts a second and less painful severance from the mother by a phantastic reproduction of the primal situation.   On the other hand, the motive of the two mothers, which Jung interprets as a symbol of rebirth, refers, through its characterization of them as mother and nurse (fed by animals), directly to the second trauma of weaning.   Authentic reminiscences of the two experienced primal traumata are, therefore, at the bottom of myths exactly as they are of neuroses.   This may be illustrated by a short reference to the Heracles myth, which expressly reports how *difficult the birth of Heracles was*.   And it is described in detail that, when he, as a suckling, was exposed by his mother, namely, expelled from the womb, he was taken by the mother goddess Hera herself to her breast.   But the vigorous boy caused her such pain (as the Saga further relates) that she angrily threw the child to the ground.[1] One could scarcely expect a clearer recollection of these earliest traumata even in analyses unless it were in the form of neurotic reproductions which, however, are manifested in the heroic over-compensation as heroic deeds.

The typical reaction to the primal trauma is shown more

how this weak point can later become a " symbolic " representative for one's own genitals (foot =penis, castration fear).

Also Adler's theory of organ inferiority and its over compensation (Achilles is called " swift-footed "), which the author attempts to establish as an embryological inheritance, seems individually rooted in the reaction to the birth trauma.

[1] *Cf. The Myth of the Birth of the Hero*, where similar traditions are quoted.

Also Achilles, the later hero of the Æolian emigrants, shows in his name the signs of the weaning trauma; he is called the Lip-less (*acheilos*), because his mother had burnt his lip in the fire where she put him in order to make him immortal.

naïvely in *children's fairy tales* than in the hero formation, stamped as is the latter with the mark of mythical compensation; especially in those fairy tales in which the hero himself, while still a child, is represented as a kind of passive hero. Besides the already analytically valued birth fairy tale of " Little Red Riding Hood," which does not forget even the asphyxia of the child cut out from the wolf's belly, and the congestion of blood to the head (red hood), (and its variations, " The Seven Kids " and others),[1] mention may be made here of the fairy tale of Hänsel and Gretel, perhaps the clearest representation of the birth theme. This again portrays the evil primal mother (witch) as an animal which swallows the children, and shows how the post-natal situation of bodily need (hunger)[2] is continually replaced by new representations of the womb and its unstinting supply of food;

[1] See my *Psychoanalytische Beiträge zur Mythenforschung*, 2nd edition, p. 67.

[2] I must here leave it an open question as to how far the primeval trauma of the *Ice Age*, which may be represented in the myth of the Flood, finds a close parallel and explanation in the primal ontogenetic trauma of the *individual*. The Unconscious still knows the sudden changes of temperature, the opposites of warm and cold, as typical reproductions of the birth trauma, represented in the dream as in certain neurotic vaso-motor disturbances, as shivering and blushing, etc. In any case, this individual experience seems to have been not without its influence on our *idea* of the Ice Age, the scientific conception of which is in no way yet proved. Probably it is a question of not one but several slowly advancing cooling periods which the individual, moreover, could not have perceived at all. However, by means of Ferenczi's bioanalytic theory of catastrophes both conceptions could be united on the ground of phylogenesis.

Fuhrmann notices that fairy tales originally were winter tales, that is, they were told only in winter in order to give consolation through the long dark months (*Das Tier in der Religion*, Munich, 1912, p. 53). One can also there compare his interpretation of the Danish Saga of King Lindwurm (Dragon) in the meaning of birth (p. 51 ff.).

such as the Utopian motive of the edible house, or the cage where one is so richly fed that one has finally to escape, but only to come back again into the hot baking-oven.[1]

A second type of fairy tale no longer presents the child in his direct reactions to the birth trauma, but as the matured youth in his love life. These popular narratives of the successful fairy prince,[2] who rescues the virgin destined for him and wins her against the opposition of all his rival brothers, are, in our view, to be understood in relation to the sexual trauma, namely, as the reaction of the primal libido to heterosexuality.

Whereas in the birth myth the hero is saved by the mother —that is, hidden in the womb, away from the father[3]—in order later, as a social and ethical reformer, to enforce progressive civilization against the older father generation,[4] the family romance of the fairy Prince reveals to us the rescue of the mother (or daughter figure) from the power of an evil tyrant as a motive of revenge. But the typical *fairy tales of deliverance* disclose to us how he is in the position to do this and what the fearless victory over all these terrifying adventures ultimately signifies. The typical details of the

[1] The well-known birth symbolism of bread and baking, which Fuhrmann has recently presented (see *Der Sinn im Gegenstand*, p. 6).

[2] Moreover, the " Family Romance," forming a basis for the hero myths and quite naïvely appearing in the fairy tales, besides its conscious ennobling tendency and the unconscious aversion to the father, has the final meaning of cancelling one's own birth.

[3] The type of legends of cannibalism. Attempts at its analysis in my treatise, " Die Don Juan-Gestalt " (*Imago*, viii., 1922).

[4] As " founder of a town " he attempts to materialize anew the primal situation of the material protection.

Even in the Psychogenesis of intellectual reformers, of the mental hero, as perhaps represented most clearly by Nietzsche, we recognize in the " freeing " from all traditions and conventions the same tendency towards detachment.

deliverance show very clearly that the rescue of the woman from the *sleep of death* represents nothing else than the revaluation of one's own birth by means of the " heroic lie." The difficulty and danger of coming out is therefore replaced by the difficulty of going in or penetrating—for example, the thorns around the Sleeping Beauty, the flames surrounding Brunnhilde, climbing slippery glass mountains or passing through closing rocks, etc.   The final breaking of the protective covering, is represented by the splitting of armour, the opening of coffins, or the ripping open of garments, in which the girl appears to be enclosed.   That all these actions are also obviously symbols of defloration, only strengthens the idea that coitus itself is only concerned with remodelling in a pleasurable way the going into the mother, so that the physiological ideal of virginity proves to be not merely a renunciation but also a direct substitution for the mother ideal.[1]   The fact, important for the understanding of fairy tales, that behind the genital signification of symbols there is also the birth signification,[2] refers further to the double quality of pleasure and pain in parturition, and shows how the anxiety arising from the birth trauma can be overcome by " redeeming " love.   So it follows that the rescue of the sleeping woman by the fearless hero has as its foundation the denial of the birth anxiety.   This is clearly shown in those tales where the hero, after slaying the dragon

[1] The penetration is the more pleasurable the more it brings to remembrance the difficulties of coming out.   On the other hand, the virginity decreases the primal anxiety, since no one can have yet been inside.   *Cf.* also Freud's treatise, " The Taboo of Virginity," *Coll. Papers*, vol. iv., 1918.

[2] As an example of this, one would like to say " phylogenetic " symbolism may be proved from the fairy tale of the *Frog-Prince*, where the frog represents not only penis but also fœtus.

from which he rescues the virgin,[1] himself falls into a death-like sleep during which his head is cut off and afterwards is put on again back to front (birth situation).[2] The death-like sleep, as in all states of hypnosis, stiffness (turning into stone), etc., but likewise in dreams and all neurotic and psychotic conditions, is therefore reproduced as a typical detail of the intrauterine situation.[3]

This also makes it clear why it must always be *the youngest* who appears as the hero in preference to his brothers. His attachment to the mother does not merely rest on the psychical motives of tenderness and pampering (mother's little son), for this itself has a biological founda-tion. Physically he remains as it were permanently attached to her, because no one after him has occupied the place, in the mother (motive of virginity). Thus he is really the only one for whom return to the womb and remaining there would be possible, for whom it is, so to say, a reward. The elder brothers, indeed, seek vainly to dispute his place, which in spite of his characteristic " stupidity " he struggles for and maintains.[4] His superiority really consists in the fact that

[1] In Babylonian cosmology, the world is made from the monster Tiamat's body, which has been cut in two.
[2] For instance, in the " Brother fairy tales." See my *Psycho-analytische Beiträge zur Mythenforschung*, 2nd edition, chap. vi., p. 119 ff.
[3] Here fits in the theme of fertilization (coitus) in sleep, portrayed in the form of anecdote or novel.
[4] This foolishness, which is always portrayed as sexual inexperience (Parsifal sleeps several nights beside his beloved without touching her) seems to correspond to the original situation of libido gratifica-tion, as the African narratives which Frobenius heard from the Hamites in the Nile district show. There a king's son frequently sleeps for months at a time with a princess, every night " they embrace with their legs " and " suck constantly at the lips." After months the discovery follows. The prince is sacrificed within an

he comes last, and, so to say, drives the others away. In this he is like the father, with whom he alone, and from the same motives, is able to identify himself.

To the same type of deliverance myths belongs also the biblical *Legend of Paradise* where, as a direct reversal of the real occurrence, the woman is cut out of the man, that is, the man is born " like a hero," because there it is he who falls into the death-like sleep.[1] The ensuing expulsion from Paradise, which has become for all of us the symbol of the unattainable blessed primal condition, represents once again a repetition of painful parturition, the separation from the mother by the father to which men and women are subjected in the same way. The curse following on the original sin of birth, " In pain shalt thou bring forth thy children," clearly divulges the motive lying at the bottom of the entire myth formation, which is, namely, to make of no effect the primal trauma whose unavoidable continuous repetition is expressed in the fruit simile. The command not to eat of the fruit of the tree of Paradise shows the same unwillingness, in the sense of the birth trauma, to separate the ripe fruit from the maternal stem as, in the myth of the birth of the hero, the original hostility of the father to the hero's coming into the world at all. Also the death punishment decreed for the breaking of this command clearly shows that the woman's offence consists in *the breaking off of the fruit*, namely, giving birth, and here again in the

---

inch of his life. Then his position is revealed, the marriage is celebrated and consummated, and on the wedding night " he found an unpierced mussel shell and blood-stains on the sheet " (*Das Unbekannte Afrika*, p. 77).

[1] The breathing of breath into the nostrils again refers to the accompanying dyspnœa of the newly born. The later Greek and New Testament pneuma doctrine has its root here.

meaning of the tendency to return death proves to be a wish-reaction to the birth trauma.

As I have already broadly indicated in *The Myth of the Birth of the Hero* and fully stated in the *Lohengrinsage*, this idea is valid for all mythical traditions of the death of the hero, and is revealed in the manner of his dying and in the burial customs of all peoples and periods, in a way that is often surprising to our minds, but quite familiar to our Unconscious. It is in no way determined, as Jung concluded from the mani-fest content, by the idea of rebirth, burdened from the begin-ning with the curse of death (reincarnation), but is to be understood from the Unconscious concept of death itself as an everlasting return to the womb. Everyone born sinks back again into the womb from which he or she once came into the realm of light, roused by the deed of man. Indeed, the ancients recognized in this taking back of the dead the highest expression of mother love which keeps faith with her offspring at the moment when it stands there abandoned by all (Bachofen).[2] Bachofen has demonstrated this very beautifully in the death-bringing Nemesis springing from

[1] In the Polar zone the dead are placed in a squatting attitude in a prismatic receptacle with a skin drawn over it; similarly also in ancient Egypt before the time of embalming, in a crouching position, wrapped in a skin (Fuhrmann, *Der Grabbau*). In New Guinea the burial places were underneath the women's houses. In later civiliza-tion the dead man's wife was buried with him or, if he was unmarried, a widow or young girl was sacrificed, later to be replaced by the so-called " concubines of the dead " (naked female clay figures) (*Hand-wörte der Sex. Wiss.*).

[2] *Oknos der Seilflechter. Erlösungsgedanken antiker Gräbersym-bolik* (new edition, Munich, 1923, p. 81). The *Oknos Motif* belongs to the series of those underworld works which we shall understand in the next chapter as the conversion of the primal pleasurable situation into a painful one; he twists unceasingly a *rope*, the other end of which is swallowed by a she-ass (attachment to the umbilical cord).

the (bird's) egg,[1] as well as in a number of other ancient goddesses of the underworld and of death. "We see how this point of view required throughout a she-ass and (in the Oknos myth) a female Typho, and we recognize the close connection that unites the she-ass with the egg-shaped mother of death on the Lycian Harpy monuments, with the burial of the King's daughter in the body of the cow expressly made for that purpose (Herod., 2, 131), with the sterile and deathly character of the Gorgonic Minerva, with the representation of huge grave mothers, and with the Demetrian naming of the dead. Everywhere Woman appears as bearer of the law of death, and, in this identification, at the same time appears as affectionate and as a dark threatening power, capable of the deepest sympathy but also of the greatest severity, like the maternally formed Harpies and the Egyptian-Phœnician Sphinx who bore in herself the law of all material life" (Oknos, p. 83). According to Bachofen, this also explains why men were excluded from the ancient rites of mourning (cf. the "Wailing Women" at Hector's corpse, and the mourning women at the foot of the cross), and the "female" death ceremonial, as it survives even in the superstitions of the German people in isolated unintelligible rites; for example, the southern German corpse-boards, which have no other purpose than to enable the dead to touch the maternal wood; further, carrying the corpse feet first from the house—thus in the reversed birth position—and pouring out water behind it (amniotic fluid).[2]

[1] "On the Lycian Harpy monument the egg itself forms the bird's body. Egg and hen here occur together. What the myth places together through the representation of the daughter (Leda) and the mother relation, plastic art gives in more complete form" (Mutterrecht, p. 70 ff.)

[2] According to Lorenz, l.c., p. 75. See also the sentence from the Rigveda (x., 18, 49, and 50), pronounced beside the grave, to the

How this simple mythical mother symbol becomes transformed into the picture of everlasting punishment characteristic of religion Bachofen has shown in a particularly beautiful manner in the Danaïdes Myth (*Oknos*, p. 89 ff.). So if even the death punishment, which in the biblical narrative repeats and inflicts the expulsion from Paradise, finally seems to be the most definite wish fulfilment of the Unconscious, this is in complete harmony with the infantile conception of dying, namely, a return to the place from where one came. In the legends of Paradise and the Golden Age we have before us a description of this primal condition, with emphasis laid on the pleasurable side of it, whilst the great systems of religion, dualistic from the beginning in the meaning of the compulsion-neurotic ambivalence, represent the ethical reaction-formations against the breaking out of this fearful yearning to go back, and the attempts to sublimate it.

---

earth: " Creep now into mother earth, into the very spacious, wide and most holy. Soft as wool is the earth to the one who offers up the sacrifice, it protects thee on thy further journey. . . . Lift thyself up, O thou spacious one; *press not downwards, be easily accessible to him and easily approachable. As the mother covers the son* with the corner of her garment, cover him also, O Earth."

RELIGIOUS SUBLIMATION

EVERY form of religion tends ultimately to the creation of a succouring and protecting primal Being to whose bosom one can flee away from all troubles and dangers and to whom one finally returns in a future life which is a faithful, although sublimated, image of the once lost Paradise. This tendency is most consistently developed in the Christian mythology, summing up and embracing the entire view of the ancient world. Christian mythology with its richly peopled heaven represented a re-humanizing of the ancient Oriental mythology of heaven; to which, at a later stage of repression, was linked the *astrology* of the Middle Ages, with its *birth-horoscopes*,[1] and which finally emerged as scientific astronomy, though still containing a wealth of unconscious phantastic elements.

How the ancient world picture, culminating in the Babylonian world view, finally developed only a real psychological analysis could teach us. For as far back as tradition goes, even presented in sculpture, we see only an apparently accomplished purely astral world picture, about the origin of which the Babylonian tradition itself gives no information. A more recent attempt of this kind by Hermann Schneider, to establish a " neolithic " Sun-worship in the earliest Babylonian and Egyptian[2] religion, seems to me to

[1] One might even describe astrology as the first doctrine of the birth trauma. The entire being and fate of man is determined by what occurs (in heaven) *at the moment of his birth.*

[2] *Die jungsteinliche Sonnenreligion im ältestesten Babylonien und Ägypten*, Leipzig, 1923. (*Mitteilungen der Vorderasiatisch-Ägyptischen Gesellschaft*, 1922, 3, 27, Jahrgang.)

have failed in so far as the learned author is too ready to find what he is looking for, and by so doing frequently neglects the meaning of the material. But in any case it is a fact that the material given by him, from the pre-Babylonian seal-pictures, existed about 4000 B.C. Here we already see before us as a finished product (*l.c.*, p. 11) "the entire symbolism of neolithic Sun-religion, as known from the Northern rock drawings." Only when one takes as much trouble over the psychical origin as one takes over the historical is one in a position to grasp the whole problem of the *development* of this neolithic Sun-religion.

The astral world view which meets us in this apparently completed form is, as I shall show in detail elsewhere, the late product of a long psychical process of projection, on which, in the course of the following arguments, some light will be thrown. Here it will be sufficient to emphasize the fact that, according to Schneider's view, this entire development " may have started from the high valuation of fire " which " exists as sun in the heavens," as it " is present in the warm bodies of men and animals " (*l.c.*, p. 4). As the maternal origin of the worship of the sun is thus obvious, a simple juxtaposition of the " cult of the stars " of primitive folks, for example, the Cora-Indians, may serve to show how these " religious " ideas also have their roots in the relation of the child to the mother. The starry heaven is there identified with the underworld, as night prevails in both places. Thus it is the place of Death. The stars in this connection are the dead ancestors who appear in the night sky at the same time as they enter the underworld. But as all vegetation grows up from the underworld, the night sky, which is a reflection of the underworld, is likewise a place of fertility.[1] In the

---

[1] Preuss, *Nayarit Expedition*, pp. xxvii and xxx (quoted by Storch, *l.c.*).

old Mexican myths the stars were designated as sacrifices, serving the purpose of nourishment for the setting sun who could not renew himself without this food. The earthly human sacrifices, as Preuss argues, are to a great extent only imitations of this sacrifice of the star deities (*l.c.*, p. 35).

Quite apart from, indeed directly opposed to, this ancient projection into the macrocosm, is the development of the other large branch of ancient Oriental religion: the old Hindu mystic doctrine of meditation directed into the human microcosm. And there in the doctrine of the transmigration of the soul it reaches the highest point in the victory over the birth trauma. F. Alexander, in an excellent study[1] based on Heiler's[2] presentation, has recently shown up the pronounced " therapeutic " character of this religiously coloured philosophy and ethic, the " Yoga practice," and has there alluded[3] to its similarity to analytic procedure. The aim of all these practices is Nirvana, the pleasurable Nothing, the womb situation, to which even Schopenhauer's half metaphysical " Will " yearned solely to return. The way to it, as in analysis, is the putting oneself into a dreamy attitude of meditation approaching the embryonal condition, the result of which, according to Alexander, actually makes

[1] " Der biologische Sinn psychischer Vorgänge. Eine psycho-analytische Studie über Buddhas Versenkungslehre," *Imago*, ix., 1, 1923. Congress lecture, Berlin, September, 1922.

[2] *Die Buddhistische Versenkung*, Munich, 1922.

[3] Recent attempts, such as that of Oscar A. H. Schmitz, to combine Psychoanalysis and Yoga, bear evidence only of the insufficient psychological conception of both phenomena, for these can replace one another only in a certain sense. The tendency to modernize ancient forms of overcoming the birth trauma betrays only the indestructible character of the regression pressure, the source of which, moreover, Schmitz approaches at one point in his presentation, in making use of psychoanalytic ideas (*Psychoanalyse und Yoga*, Darmstadt, 1923, p. 89)

possible an extensive reminiscence of the intrauterine situation.

To Hauer's[1] recently published investigations we owe our access to the ancient Hindu descriptions of ecstatic experiences, which allow the meaning of all these preparations to be clearly recognized. The pupil of the sacred Brahmins, the Brahmacarin who tries to absorb the secret magic power, which for the Hindu means the primal cause of Being, during his initiation (*Upanayana*) must experience in the teacher's womb an hypnotic sleep condition lasting for three days. " The teacher who initiates the pupil makes of him an embryo in his inmost parts. Three nights he carries him in *the womb*. Then he brings forth him who comes to see the Gods " (*Atharvaveda*, xi., 5, according to Hauer, p. 86). As Oldenburg has ascertained for the so-called *Diksa* (holy sacrifice), the novitiate probably sat for three days in a hut, with clenched fists and legs bent upwards in the embryonal position, surrounded with all kinds of coverings (amnion) (Hauer, p. 98). " The priests convert that one with whom they consummate the diksa again into an embryo. The hut of sacrifice is for the Diksita (the one offering the sacrifice) the womb; thus they allow him to enter the womb again; they cover him with a robe. The robe is for the Diksita the amnion; thus they surround him with the amnion. A black antelope skin is placed above, outside the amnion is the Chorion (cloak or mantle); thus they cover him with the Chorion. He clenches his fists. With clenched fists lies the embryo inside; with clenched fists the boy is born— putting aside the black antelope skin he descends to an underground room (Avabhrthabad); for that reason the

---

[1] *Die Anfänge der Yogapraxis : eine Untersuchung über die Wurzeln der indischen Mystik*, 1922.

embryos are born free of the Chorion. With his robe he descends; for that reason is the boy born with the amnion."[1] There is clearly described in the Rigveda a position, *uttana,* which has been preserved in the present-day Yoga practices, and which as Storch (*l.c.*, p. 78) remarks, "is similar to certain embryonal positions, as we see them not infrequently in the stereotyped position of catatonics." In other places of the Rigveda are mentioned rolling movements of the head and eyes, swinging motions, tremblings and rockings to and fro, all of which again seem to relate to the birth trauma.

We have before us here the primal phenomenon of the pleasurable-protecting situation. From this there later emerges, through severance from the mother and transference to the father, the figure of the almighty and all-loving, but also punishing, God, as a religious sublimation by means of projection. As Rudolph Otto thinks,[2] there exist as the origin of all historical religions, before the development of definitely outlined forms of demons and gods, certain " nebulous primal feelings," feelings of shuddering before the gruesome, of marvelling at the mysterious, manifested at first in the primitives as " fear of demons."[3] We now know through Freud's explanations[4] that the demons relate originally to the fear of the dead, that is, they correspond to the feeling of guilt projected outwards, whilst on the other hand the indefinite anxiety itself, as exhibited

[1] Oldenburg, *Religion des Veda*, second edition, p. 405.

[2] *Das Heilige. Über das Irrationale in der Idee des Göttlichen und sein Verhältnis zum Rationalen,* 11th edition, Stuttgart, 1923.

[3] The positive side of this religious primal feeling, the " mystical continuous-power" subsisting between all human beings and things, and conceived as active under the names *Orenda, Wakondo, Mana,* has been recognized by Lorenz as projection of the mother-child relation (*l.c.*, p. 58 ff.).

[4] *Totem und Taboo,* 1912, p. 13.

in the child, is to be explained as a continuance of the primal trauma. It becomes clear from the development of the individual that the primal fear is again directly linked up with the dead, representing the pre-natal situation. The steps leading from belief in demons to belief in gods have been well investigated both in mythology and folklore. But the psychological factor of the entire development lies in the gradual substitution of the mother (demons), to whom anxiety clings by the form of the father appealing to the sublimated anxiety, the guilt feeling. This process of religious development runs absolutely parallel with that of social development as we have described it (pp. 89-93). Here also there appears at the beginning the cult of the great Asiatic mother goddess, who is regarded sometimes as the wild, sensuous goddess of love and of the fertility of Nature in general, sometimes as the pure queen of heaven, the virgin goddess,"[1] who appears again in Eve and Mary, and is continued in the Charis of Irenæus, in the Helena of Simon Magnus, in Sophia and others. "A sublime flexibility," says a recent investigator of the ' Gnostic Mysteries,'[2] " is manifested in the belief in the mother goddess. In it positively everything which was religious in any sense or kind found a place, from orgies, æsthetic and artistic tendencies, from the Mysteries of συνουσία to astrology and the star of Bethlehem. The mother goddess could be everything, the world soul, world mind, world development, world pleasure, world pain, and world deliverance, world light, world seed, world sin, and everything in which may be seen in successive stages a reflection of Being, even down

[1] See Bousset in *Realenzyklopädie von Pauly-Wissowa-Kroll*, vii., 1513 ff.

[2] *Ein Beitrag zur Geschichte des christlichen Gottesdienstes*, by Dr. Leonhard Fendt, Munich, 1922, p. 41.

to the very vegetables.   She could be laughter and weeping, mind and body, goddess and demon, heaven, earth, and hell." As Winterstein has already recognized, the later religious and philosophic ideas of a creation of the world by a male god are only the result[1] of a renunciation of the primal

[1] Yet in the Christian religion God is provided with a uterus. In Petavius, *de Trinitate*, lib. v., chap. 7, 4, it is written: " Even so, says the writing, the Son is begotten of the Father from the uterus: although in God there is no uterus, moreover nothing physical, yet in him there is a real creation, a real birth which is shown even in the word ' uterus ' " (quoted by Winterstein, *l.c.*, p. 194).

Further, relevant and intensely interesting material appears in Wolfgang Schultz, *Dokumente der Gnosis*, Jena, 1910.

I cannot refrain here from quoting the chief idea and some sentences from the wonderful " Buch von der Schöpfung des Kindes," as it stands in the *Kleine Midraschim*. The " Book " begins with the cohabitation of the parents, and with the first adventures of the " drop," which is guarded by an angel. After " the soul " is brought to the drop, the Angel of Morning leads it into Paradise, and the Angel of Evening leads it into " hell " and then shows it the place where it will dwell on earth, and the place where it will be buried. " But the Angel leads it back again into the body of its mother, and the Holy One, praise be to him, makes doors and bolts for it.   And the Holy One, praise be to him, says to it, ' As far as this shalt thou come and no further.'   And the child lies in the womb of its mother nine months. . . .   The first three months it dwells in the lowest chamber, the three middle months in the centre chamber, and the three last months in the uppermost chamber.   And it eats of everything which its mother eats, and drinks of all which its mother drinks, and excretes no dirt; otherwise would its mother die.   And as soon as that time is come when it must go out, the first Angel comes and says to it, ' Go out, for the time is come when you must go out into the world.'   And the spirit of the child answers, ' Before him who spoke and the world was, I have already said that I am satisfied with the world in which I have lived.'   And the Angel answers, ' The world into which I bring you is beautiful.'   And again, ' Against your Will have you been formed in your mother's womb, *and against your Will, shall you be born*, to go out into the world.'   Immediately the child *weeps*.   And why does it weep ? Just because of that world in which it was and which it now leaves.

mother, such as is to be found in the biblical creation of man. Corresponding to this we find the heretical sects, as well of the Jewish as of the Christian belief, characterized by a sexually emphasized return to the mother goddess. These revolutionary movements within religion thus proceed entirely along the same way as in the social movements, namely, the way of regression to the mother.

Thus the well-known cult of the sperm in the Gnostic Eucharist of the sect of the Phibionites (about A.D. 200-300) seems to be connected with the service of the Asiatic-Egyptian mother goddess called Mani by the Sumerians, Ishtar in Babylon, Magna Mater, Cybele, Ma, Ammas in Asia Minor, the Great Mother in Carthage, Isis in Egypt, Demeter among the Greeks, Astarte among the Syrians, Anahita among the Persians, Alilat among the Nabateans, Kwannyin in the Indian, Kwannon in Japanese Buddhism, and the "Primal Mother" in Chinese Taoism. The Phibionite meal, this *religio libidinum*, which "in spite of all the real heathenism in it, still consists essentially, as the old abstruse commentaries on the Christian Last Supper and its derivative the Mass assume,"[1] and, as Fendt rightly recognized (*l.c.*, 4), not in sexual intercourse, which was so much urged against it as a reproach,[2] but in eating (devour-

---

And as *it goes out, the Angel strikes it under its nose* and blots out the light over its head. *He brings it out against its will and it forgets everything which it has seen.* And as it comes out it weeps."

[1] See Fendt, *Gnostische Mysterien, l.c.*, p. 8.

[2] Especially the incestuous orgies which belong equally to the Asiatic cult of the mother (see Rank, *Inzestmot.*, iv., 1912) as to the Devil's Mass, in which a woman again is adored (*cf.* Lowenstein, " Zur Psychologie der Schwarzen Messen," *Imago*, ix., 1923).

Minucius Felix (about 200) reproaches the Phibionites with: " Post multas epulas, ubi convivium caluit et incestæ libidinis ebriatis fervo exarsit " (Fendt, *l.c.*, 12).

ing) the sexual excreta. "The woman and the man take the sperm in their hands. . . . And so they eat it and communicate their own disgrace and say: This is the body of Christ. . . . But they do likewise with that of the woman, when the woman is menstruating . . . and they eat of it likewise in common. And they say: ' *This is the blood of Christ.*' "[1] Fendt sees logically (*l.c.*, 5) in the third feast, which is called " the perfect Pasha," the supplement and explanation of the other two in the sense that the sexual act is used only for the purpose of destroying the semen, the sole means of the Archon of Desire. " If, in spite of all, a child is begotten, then the child is to be the sacred food of the third meal! From every woman thus accidentally made a mother, the embryo is cut out, torn to pieces, and prepared with honey, pepper, oil and perfumes, and every one eats of it with the finger. . . . And afterwards as a thank-offering they say these words: ' The master (Archon) of Desire was unable to fool us, no, we have gathered up the brother's transgression.' " "Now," Fendt adds (p. 5), interpreting, " we are familiar with a kind of struggle against the Archons in the form of a breaking of the commandment which Clement of Alexandria reports of the Antitaktes and Nikolaitans in this way: all which *God the father* created was good; but an Under-God mixed evil with it; from this Under-God came the command . . . the Archon of Desire wills that children be created . . . therefore everything is done to prevent the begetting of children."

We have related in detail this cult and its commentaries, because in it the whole mechanism of religious sublimation, thus the real formation of religion, is revealed undisguised.

[1] For a similar comparison of the Great Mother with Christ as the Logos, see Fendt, p. 80.

The evil Under-God, who brings children into the world thus compelling them continuously to endure the birth trauma, is the mother; and the entire (incestuous) unchastity of the Gnostics amounts simply to going back again into the mother's womb, and thereby excluding the renewal of the birth trauma; this is why the semen is assimilated through the mouth (eaten). Should, however, conception result, then the embryo is cut out in order to prevent the trauma, and again assimilated only through the mouth. Fendt says: " The world development is comprehended as an enormous failure; salvation comes only through *withdrawal* of that which is All Effective in the Universe."[1]

The father-God has been put in the place of the primal mother charged with anxiety and desire, in order, in the Freudian meaning of " Totemism," to create and to guarantee social organization. Every relapse to the veneration of the mother, which can only be accomplished sexually, is therefore anti-social and is persecuted with all the horror of so-called religious fanaticism.[2] But this, like social revolution, finally results in the preservation and strengthening of the father-like power for the protection of the social community. For this reason, all such movements of reversion are

[1] Also the Brahmin pupil who suffers loss of semen prays: " To me *return* again Sensual-power, Life, and Blessing, to me come back again my Brahmanship, my Property. The semen which today from me has slipped to earth, which has escaped to the herbs, to the waters, *I receive again into myself* for long Life and Splendour " (Oldenburg, *l.c.*, 430). Of the Yogi it is said: " By practice he compels *the drop which wants to enter into the womb of the woman, to return.* But if a single drop *has already fallen*, he forces it to *return to him* and he keeps it. The Yogi who thus maintains the drop, will *conquer death.* For as the fallen drop signifies death, even so its preservation signifies Life " (Schmidt, *Fakir und Fakirtum*, 1908).

[2] See Reik concerning this theme, " Der eigene und der fremde Gott." *Zur Psychoanalyse der religiösen Entwicklung*, 1923.

followed by an increased puritanical reaction, as we can see in the history of the Jewish belief. The best-known movement of this kind is the pseudo-messianic period of the " Schabbatianians," about 300 years ago, whose founder, Schabbethai Z'evi, was a Spanish Jew from Smyrna.[1] Like the Gnostics, he also proclaimed a breaking of the command-ment, and his disciples then—especially after his death—broke away completely from the puritanical laws of Judaism. The peculiarity of this movement consisted in the fact that *woman was the deity*, and forbidden forms of the sexual life, especially the incestuous, were esteemed divine service. " In caves in the neighbourhood of Salonika they organized the wildest orgies for religious purposes. At the beginning of the Sabbath they placed a naked virgin in their midst and likewise naked danced around her. Orgies were substituted for prayer. Similar customs spread throughout nearly all Jewish communities of the world. Naturally they were most severely persecuted by the Rabbis. Nevertheless they failed for 200 years to exterminate the sect. In Turkey there are remains of it even to the present day " (Langer, *l.c.*, p. 39). The direct reaction, which according to Langer's ingenious explanation led not only to the ascetic exclusion of woman but to an increase of socially effective homo-sexuality,[2] is linked to the name of the famous Rabbi Israel ben Elieser, Baal Schem Tow (1700-1760), and to the Has-sidism created by him. Langer comes to the conclusion that " the entire inner history of the chosen people appears really as a chain of more or less conscious battles in two

[1] According to Georg Langer, *Die Erotik der Kabbala*, Prague, 1923.
[2] Deuteronomy (xiii. 7) speaks of the " friend who is to you as your soul," and directly after of " the woman of thy womb " as of something quite generally known (Langer, p. 91).

directions. The battle was generally terminated by a compromise, which in prehistoric times added new laws and new symbols to those already existing. In this Freud's so-called Œdipus complex and the conception of death are powerful forces, and thus the whole Jewish legislation is really performed by Eros, before it obtained its godly sanction through revelation " (*l.c.*, p. 93).

To this excellent definition we would like to join a methodological remark, which also has reference to the psychoanalytic investigation of religion. There is no doubt that in these maternal sects and cults we have to deal with phenomena of reversion in the sense of a " return of the repressed." But here, as in the biological sphere, one must be on one's guard against an untimely introduction of the phylogenetic point of view, as also against the attempt to find or to reconstruct an historical basis, where in any case it is a question of a psychological basis, though this is certainly in the Unconscious. Thus the modern Jewish sectarians apparently go back to the Asiatic cult of the mother, although naturally they need know nothing at all of it, but are simply producing the same reactions from their Unconscious individually experienced. But cases where direct borrowing is possible or even probable, as in the Jewish "golden calf,"[1] which seems to represent " the new-born " as Son-God, are psychologically more important and more interesting than that of the " tradition " which is always only mechanical. If in the tradition of the father-religion itself, on the other hand, we are enabled to reconstruct and to recognize fragments of the repressed preliminary stages of the mother-

[1] " Idolatry " seems to signify simply service to the mother deity. *Cf.* the service of Baal (Canaan, El) to whom among the Phœnicians and other people little children were thrown into the fiery mouth of the idol.

religion, we shall have to hold fast to the fact that these are only *preliminary stages in the formation of religion*, in the real meaning of the word, and must, as Freud[1] has pointed out, be regarded as the *final result* of primal battles for and against the mother and as the victory of the social power of the father.

From this point of view, besides the social development of the " horde of brothers " into the community, described by Freud, we can also trace its religious development a little further and, indeed, in harmony with our assumption of social development (king-infant) as the transition of the mother-cult to the father-religion, by means of the Son-Godhead, which has found in Christianity its purest expression. It may be, moreover, that the world-wide historical importance of Christianity rests on the fact that it was the first to place the Son-God in the centre without simultaneously attacking the original rights of the mother and the secondary rights of the father. The high valuation placed on the child by Christ in the text of the Gospels would further agree with this. Christ himself has ever remained an *infant*, even as sculpture represents him, when dead (Pieta).

In the ancient mysteries *every single mystic himself became directly a God*. The formula of confession: " I have fasted, I have drunk the mixed drink (*Kikeon*), I have taken it out of the box, and after I worked, I laid it in the basket and from the basket into the box," shows that we are here concerned with regression (and return) into the womb, which the *cysta mystica* (holy box) is now held to represent even by the archæologists. " In taking from the holy box (χιογη) the image of a womb and slipping it over his body,

---

[1] *Totem und Taboo.*

9

the mystic is assured of being reborn from the womb of the earth mother, and of becoming her bodily child."[1]   This also explains the still more obscure allusions in which many Christian writers spoke of the secret of the Eleusinian Mysteries: " Is there not *the dark descent* and the imposing companionship of the Hierophant and the Priestess, between him and her alone, and does not a numerous multitude consider holy what is consummated between the two in the dark."[2]   It is not a question of mere coitus nor even of a "sacred one, in which 'a numerous crowd' can be participators, but it is a matter of union with the mother. This is proved not only by the symbol *cysta mystica* but still more clearly by the realistic Phrygian mystery cult, in which the mystic descends into a grave, ' where the *blood* of a slaughtered bull is *poured* over him.   After the rebirth he receives *milk nourishment* as the God in him or he in the God *is yet a child*, then he steps up and is worshipped as God by the community.'[3]   The Hindu Yoga practice through mystical meditation likewise enables *each individual himself to become God*—that is, by entering the womb, by being transformed back into the embryo, he participates in the god-like omnipotence " (see Ferenczi, *Stages in the Development of the Sense of Reality*).

So the *infans*—ultimately the unborn—proves to be God, like his earthly substitutes, whether king or Pope,

[1] A. Korte, in *Arch. f. Rel. Wiss.*, xviii., 1915.

[2] De Jong, *Das antike Mysterienwesen*, 1909, p. 22.

[3] Reitzenstein, *Hellenistische Mysterienkulte*, 2nd edition, 1920, p. 32.   In a hermetic rebirth mystery, the mystic calls out: " I am in heaven, I am in earth, in water am I, and in the air, I am in animals, in plants, in the womb, of the womb, after the womb, I am everywhere " (*ibid.*, pp. 29 and 35).   *Cf.* also the Mysteries of the Persian Mythra and their bull sacrifice (Cumont, *Mithras*; Dietrich, *Eine Mithrasliturgie*.

RELIGIOUS SUBLIMATION 131

though subject to still greater limitations; whence it follows that each individual himself was once "God" and can be so again, if or in so far as he can reinstate himself into the primal condition, and this is the reason why each one is so easily able to identify himself with the later "one and only God."[1] But as not everyone can go back into the mother, so not everyone can be king or God. Hence the chosen of a multitude, the priests, are originally castrated; that is, they must finally renounce this privilege of going into the mother in favour of *an only one*, namely, the *youngest*, who is enabled to put himself actually in the place of the father, and by means of religious sublimation to convert the most pleasurable action, by which the crowd undoubtedly intends to punish him, into a voluntary *sacrifice* for the others.[2] In this way he saves the social community from destruction. The mother is thereby partly exalted to the queen of heaven, partly, as the evil alluring primal principle of all production, used for the formation of the religious-ethical concept of the ancient underworld, which, arising from the mythology of heaven (the beyond), leads, by way of the religious sublimation prepared for in the Johannine Apocalypse, to the other extreme of the medieval idea of hell.

In its gross physical details hell manifests itself as the fearsome counterpart to the phantasy of the intrauterine Paradise and heaven. *Eternal punishment in hell*, in par-

[1] See the same conception in the *Myth of the Birth of the Hero*, that each one is a "hero" and birth is the real achievement. When, for example, a schizophrenic (Storch, p. 60) identifies herself with Christ, since she also came into the world in a stable, she is perfectly right; for she also was born in the natural way and wants to deny the birth trauma.

[2] So Mahomet in his epileptic states (Aura) seems to have described the Islamic Paradise with its blessedness (Houri).

ticular, which corresponds to the Greek punishment in the underworld, represents in detail reproductions of the intrauterine situation (chains, heat, etc.), and it is not to be wondered at if the hysterics of the Middle Ages showed particular preference for this ready-made material in the representation of the same unconscious tendencies.[1]

The analysis of the Unconscious shows why the later lord of this " Hell " has the characteristics of the primal father, for it is he, indeed, who has reversed the original scene of all pleasurable sensations into its opposite. The original feminine signification of the devil, personified even in the mouth of hell, is perhaps still preserved in the half-comical figure of his grandmother, surviving in the witches—and not only in those in fairy tales—as the old evil and dangerous primal mother. In the medieval delusion about witches and the cruel persecutions of the Inquisition, we see the hell situation with its punishments transferred into reality, which, according to a verbally expressed conjecture of Freud's, may go back to a real trauma, which seems to me to have struck the sexual trauma and with it the birth trauma in our own Unconscious in a very direct manner.

With the interpretation of everlasting punishment as representing the intrauterine situation with negative indications, we have approached a theme already mentioned which we shall realize in the last chapter to be the psychological nuclear problem of the birth trauma. We cannot here pursue the complicated development of these primitive projections, as illuminated by the study of the compulsion neurosis, and leading eventually to highly important reaction formations which reach their climax in ethical ideas. We

---

[1] See in addition Groddeck, " Der Symbolisierungszwang," *Imago*, viii., 1922.

want only to refer to an advancing process which is therein completed and which goes parallel with an increasing insight into the psychical origin of ethical formations ultimately rooted in the unconscious guilt feeling. The higher powers who punish and reward, whom one dare not disobey, are finally transferred back again into the Ego whence they once had been projected from out of the narcissistic feeling of omnipotence into the world above and below, and there had taken shape accordingly as maternal representations (protection, help, mercy) or paternal representations (one's own feeling of omnipotence). To the rigid ethical philosophy of Kant was reserved the titanic task of once again separating the moral law in us from the starry heavens above us, and even he was only able to accomplish this by re-establishing, at least metaphorically in the well-known phrase, the identity which had been given up with such difficulty.

It is significant, for the development of the *concept of punishment*, that not only all punishments devised by mankind in phantasy, but also those converted into deed, represent the primal condition of the womb situation with emphasis laid on its painful character. Without involving ourselves in a detailed interpretation of the punishments of the Greek underworld, we need only point out that the best known of them show typical characteristics which are easily understood with reference to the locality, namely, the underworld. The crime of these primal offenders generally consists in rebellion against the highest of the gods, usually caused by the desire for his wife, the primal mother, as in the case of Ixion, who, moreover, is the first murderer of relations. His punishment consists in this: at the command of Zeus to be "bound with snakes on a winged, fiery, four-spoked wheel, which turns ceaselessly and to be rolled through the air, lashed by the scourge and the exclamation 'Benefactors should one honour.' This punishment for Ixion seems doubly hard in so far as he is immortal."[1] Similarly, Tantalus, a "personification of abundance and riches," is punished on account of his transgressing insolence towards the gods with whom he desires to be equal. The original version, in which a stone hangs above his head always threatening to fall down, shows a permanent anxiety

IXION ON THE WHEEL.
(*Picture taken from a Vase in Berlin.*)

situation; the other punishment of being eternally tormented by hunger and thirst obviously relates to the favourite who, as guest, shared in every luxurious repast of the gods, and who, in order to test the gods, placed before them human flesh. He is portrayed, moreover, on a sarcophagus (see *Roscher*, vol. v., sp. 83-84) twisted in a quite naturalistic way on a wheel, whilst Ixion is appropriately represented in a double circle. Finally Sisyphos, who also demands the same "immortality" of the gods, gets this wish fulfilled in

[1] Roscher, *Lexikon der Mythologie*, ii., 1.

the same way—namely, the eternal *rolling back* of the stone, which he attempts again and again to push over the summit of the mountain against its natural tendency to rush down: " Sweat pours from his limbs and a cloud of dust envelops his head."

But all these punishments and offenders, according to Greek tradition itself and in keeping with the development of Greek civilization, were not transferred to the place of

TANTALUS.
(*On a Sarcophagus.*)

the underworld called Tartaros until later.   Originally they were not only real and as such had the same unconscious signification, but they were again materialized in the dark Middle Ages, which compared with Hellenism itself represented a hell-like underworld. Burning and breaking of witches on the wheel—not to mention bodily dislocation of the chained and tortured (head hanging down)— blinding or exposure in water, the typical punishment

for the parricide who was sewn in a sack and sunk in the
sea:[1] all this shows quite clearly the indestructible wish-
character of the Unconscious, as Freud has recognized;
even the most horrible forms of punishment which man
could imagine and which he directs against himself in the
physical symptoms of neurosis, are clothed in the form of
the first and strongest pleasure experience of the intrauterine
life.   It is therefore possible and intelligible that punishments of this kind were not only endured but were also
pleasurably experienced, as, moreover, the habits of maso-
chists daily prove.   This explains to a large extent the
pleasurable character of certain neurotic symptoms, in
which the patient makes himself prisoner by withdrawing
into a room which he locks, or by pessimistically phantasying
the whole world as a dungeon and thereby unconsciously
feeling comfortable in it.[2]   The real punishment which
struck him long ago and from which apparently he wants
to escape through these phantasies of self-punishment, was
originally the expulsion from the womb, that primal paradise,
which is sought for again and again, with unquenchable
longing and in every possible form.

Crucifixion, which as punishment for rebellion against God
the Father stands at the centre of the Christ myth, corresponds to the same conversion and assimilation of the
intrauterine situation as the confining of Ixion in the wheel,
with the abolition of which the spokes become the cross.[3]

[1] See Storfer, *Zur Sonderstellung des Vatermordes*, 1911.

[2] From this alone the deep psychology of the so-called " Prison
Psychosis " is to be understood.

[3] Thus the cross itself still represents something " inward,"
namely, the spokes freed from the clasp of the rim.   Also the hooked
cross belongs in this connection: the spoked cross growing again
into the rim of the wheel is naturally an emblem of life and victory "
(Schneider, *l.c.*, p. 8, note 2).

Consequently crucifixion likewise corresponds to a painfully emphasized return to the womb, after which follows quite consistently the resurrection, namely, birth and not re-birth. For here it is also a question of nothing but a repetition[1] and reproduction of the process of birth, ethically and religiously sublimated in the sense of a neurotic overcoming of the primal trauma. Hence the great part which the Christian mystery of redemption plays in the phantasy life of neurotics and also of the insane is explained as identification with the passive hero who succeeds in returning to the womb by means of pleasurable suffering. This identification is a sublime attempt at recovery, which has saved mankind from the destruction of the ancient world and as such is clearly recognizable in the traditional miracles of Christ. He makes the blind and the lame healthy through his example. That is, he provokes them to identify themselves with him, because they could see in him one who had overcome the birth trauma.[2]

The infantile theory of the Immaculate Conception, as a dogmatic concept of the birth trauma, fits in unconstrainedly with this explanation of the Christ legend. It announces in the sense of the hero myth, the most extreme development of which is represented by the Christ figure, that also this negative hero, who has succeeded to a great extent in the mastery of the birth trauma, was not born in the natural way, indeed, did not even enter the mother in the natural way. This human imperfection of a severe

[1] Christ himself in the Gospels explains their untrustworthy opposition from the fact of the compulsion to repetition: " That the word of the Prophets might be fulfilled."

[2] The new era which begins with Christ's *Birth* corresponds psychologically to the embryonal year and its eternal repetition (see the Mexican parallel, p. 75, note).

birth trauma is, in harmony with our view of the determination of neurotic symptoms, made good to a certain extent in the later life of the adult by the latter's physical and psychical sufferings. In this way the manifest punishment represents, according to its latent content, the ideal wish fulfilment, namely, the return into the mother, whilst the artistic idealization of the crucified Saviour expresses, according to its latent meaning, the real punishment of the underworld, the prevention of the embryonal position.

LUKAS CRANACH. CRUCIFIXION.

139

ARTISTIC IDEALIZATION

AN exact illustration of this all too human conception of the Christ myth is given in the realistic representation of the Crucifixion by Lukas Cranach,[1] where, by the side of the Saviour crucified in the well-known stretched-out attitude of the body, the other sinners appear nailed to the tree-stem in characteristic embryonal posture. Thus Christ's idealized position on the cross in art indicates a mechanism of defence or punishment similar to that of the *arc de cercle*. So the contrast of the realistic figures by Lukas Cranach gives a picture of the idealizing tendency of artistic representation, which seems to aim at softening, by æsthetic treatment,[2] the all too clear approach to the primal condition, lending it also the character of punishment.

In this process of artistic idealization which, in the faithful portrayal of Nature, yet aspires to æsthetic sem-

[1] There are still more realistic representations of the malefactors by Urs Graf and others.

[2] It is interesting that for Schopenhauer the essence of æsthetic achievement consisted in the deliverance from " Will." Nietzsche, who had clearly recognized the " sexual repression " working behind it (*Genealogy of Morals*, 6), quotes the well-known sentence about it (*Die Welt als Wille und Vorstellung*, i., 231: " That is the *painless condition*, which Epicurus praised as the highest good and as the condition of Gods; we are set free at that moment from contemptible will-pressure, we celebrate the sabbath of the penal-work of willing, *the wheel of Ixion stands still*." To this Nietzsche remarks: " What vehemence of words ! what pictures of torment and lasting weariness ! what almost pathological time-opposition between ' that moment ' and the eternal ' Wheel of Ixion ' ! "

blance, unreality, even a downright denial of " Nature," has found its indisputable climax in Greek civilization, the masterly psychological analysis of which Nietzsche gave for the first time. In his first work he puts forward the brilliant conception of that harmonious quality which is for us the essential factor in Greek culture and which he called "Apollonian," being the reaction against a kind of neurotic disturbance which he characterizes as "Dionysian." And he is right in instancing as the measure and standard of this process of idealization, which stands out unique in the history of the human mind, the completely changed attitude to death as expressed by the wisdom of Silenus in eulogizing the fortune of being unborn, as compared with the attitude towards life of the Homeric heroes. So that we might now say of them with a reversal of the Silenian wisdom, that[1] " to die early is worst of all for them, the second worst—some-day to die at all. . . ." "So vehemently does the will at the Apollonian stage of development long for this existence, so completely at one does the Homeric man feel himself with it, that the very lamentation becomes its song of praise. Here we must observe that this harmony so eagerly contemplated by modern man, in fact, this oneness of man with Nature, to express which Schiller introduced the technical term ' naïve,' is by no means such a simple, naturally resulting, and, as it were, inevitable condition which must be found at the gate of every culture, leading to a paradise of man. . . . Wherever we meet with the ' naïve ' in art, it behoves us to recognize the highest effect of the Apollonian culture, which in the first place has always to overthrow some titanic empire and slay monsters, and which, through powerful dazzling representations and

---

[1] *The Birth of Tragedy*, pp. 34-35; *ibid.*, pp. 36-37.

pleasurable illusions, must have triumphed over a terrible depth of world contemplation and a most keen susceptibility to suffering. . . ."

"The Greek knew and felt the terrors and horrors of existence: *to be able to live at all,* he had to interpose the shining dream-birth of the Olympian world between himself and them. The excessive distrust of the titanic powers of Nature, the Moira throning inexorably over all knowledge, the vulture of the great philanthropist Prometheus, the terrible fate of the wise Œdipus, the family curse of the Atridæ which drove Orestes to matricide; in short, that entire philosophy of the sylvan god, with its mythical exemplars, which wrought the ruin of the melancholy Etruscans — *was again and again surmounted anew* by the Greeks through the *artistic middle world* of the Olympians, or at least veiled and withdrawn from sight."[1]

In these sentences Nietzsche has, with unprecedented boldness, grasped the problem of the development of Greek culture at its very root. We need only take a short step further in psychological comprehension of the "Dionysian" and we shall stand at the original source which has fed the whole development, namely, *anxiety*! But in order now to trace the path from anxiety to art, and simultaneously to understand how the Greeks could reach the highest perfection of artistic idealization, we must go back again to the nuclear symbol of primal anxiety in its origin from the trauma of birth, namely, to *the Sphinx.*

In his suggestive book, *Das Rätsel der Sphinx*, Ludwig Laistner (1884) has connected the Greek popular legend of the monster choking human beings with the goblin legends

[1] The italics are mine.

of German tradition, and has traced both back to the human experience of the nightmare. That the anxiety dream itself reproduces the primary birth anxiety has now become psychoanalytically clear to us. Even so, the mixed figure of the Sphinx representing the anxiety experience as such has been recognized by Psychoanalysis as a mother symbol, and her character as " strangler " makes the reference to the birth anxiety unambiguous. In this meaning the rôle of the Sphinx in the Œdipus saga shows quite clearly that the hero, on the way back to the mother, has to overcome the birth anxiety, representing the barrier which the neurotic also comes up against again and again in all his attempts to regress. Reik[1] has explained very ingeniously how the Sphinx episode really represents a duplicate of the Œdipus saga itself. Only, being obviously led astray by the masculine type of the Egyptian Sphinx, which is in no way primary, although perhaps historically earlier, he wanted to prove the maternal character of the figure, originally established by Psychoanalysis, as secondary. This is proved to be untenable not merely in the connection here developed, but also in other different directions. The Œdipus saga is certainly a duplicate of the Sphinx episode, which means psychologically that it is the repetition of the primal trauma at the sexual stage (Œdipus complex), whereas the Sphinx represents the primal trauma itself. The man-swallowing character of the Sphinx brings it into direct connection with the infantile fear of animals, to which the child has that ambivalent attitude, arising out of the birth trauma, which we have already described. The hero, who is not swallowed by the Sphinx, is enabled, just through the overcoming of anxiety, to repeat the unconscious wish in the pleasurable

---

[1] " Œdipus und die Sphinx," *Imago*, vi., 1920.

form of sexual intercourse with the mother.[1] But the Sphinx, conforming to its character as strangler, represents not only in its latent content the wish to return into the mother, as the danger of being swallowed, but it also represents in its manifest form parturition itself and the struggle against it, in that the human upper body grows out of the animal-like (maternal) lower body without finally being able to free itself from it.[2] This is the riddle of the Sphinx figure,

[1] In Hesiod's *Theogony*, where the Sphinx seems first mentioned in literature, she originates from the union of Echidna, dwelling in the subterranean cave in the land of Arimi with her own son. She is also called " Offspring of Echidna of the Underworld " by Euripides (Roscher's *Lexicon*).

[2] An obvious psychological preliminary step to this is shown on the famous Terra-cotta Relief of Tenos, which portrays the Sphinx as a Goddess of Death snatching away the blossom of Youth (Roscher, iv., sp. 1,370). In addition, see the similar " Harpie des Grabmals von Xantos " in Roscher, i., p. 2, sp. 1,846). This connection of the Sphinx with death becomes easy for us to understand when we remember that the large Egyptian Sphinx of Gizeh is also nothing less than a grave, which differs from the other

SPHINX.
(*Terra-Cotta Relief from Tenos.*)

" animal coffins," as, for example, the Elephant-avenues of Ming-graves in China, only in the special combination of man and animal, that is, by emphasizing the origin of man from the animal-like body in the sense of the hero myth. The purely genital signification of the Sphinx's body (as womb) finally comes to light in the late Greek period manifestly as erotic salve receptacles for feminine use in

and in its solution lies the key to the understanding of the whole development of Greek art and culture.

If we compare even hastily the classic period of Greek art with its Oriental forerunner, we can say that the Greeks have consistently carried out the tendency to free themselves from the womb, which has found such a remarkable expres-

---

Sphinx form, as Ilberg (in Roscher's *Lexicon*, iv., sp. 1,384) describes them (for example, the beautiful Sphinx vase in the British Museum from San Maria di Capua, which Murray states to be about 440 B.C.).

We see the same in the old Peruvian ceramic art, which likewise proves that the Sphinx figure was originally a receptacle and indeed the receptacle in which the human being itself was preserved and from which he also came out. Hence the remarkable representation of a " sphinx-like " human being with the teeth of a beast of prey *under a snail's shell*, the feelers growing out of the eyes (according to Fuhrmann, *Peru*, ii., 1922, Table 57); or illustration 31 from the Hamburg Museum for Ethnology, about which Fuhrmann remarks: " A very remarkable representation with a human head which appears to grow out of the back of the animal, showing a strongly curved belly, might refer to the body of the human being still hidden inside." Illustration 30 from the Vienna Natural History Museum already approaches the Centaur type in the advanced stage of the appearing man, the psychological importance of which in our sense is supported by Fuhrmann, who points out that an animal for riding is not known in Peru, and that " the foundation for this representation has yet to be explained." In any case, the " origin " of the rider becomes intelligible, which again represents nothing else than the one united with the mother and therefore the Stronger, Higher, More Powerful, Preferred (king, leader, ruler). (When the primitive inhabitants of Mexico saw the Spanish conquerors on their horses, they thought horse and rider were one inseparable whole.) Not only do the rocking horse and hobby horse of children form the infantile example of these almost " psychotic " regressions into the animal-like body, but still more clearly does the so-called " game at horse," in which the child moves (jumps) legs and lower body in the manner of a horse, whilst the upper part of the body represents the human rider. . . . The primitive arrest in this condition is symbolized very beautifully in the " Illustrated Hallucinations " of a schizophrene, published by Bertschinger (*Jahrbuch f. Psa.*, iii., 1911).

sion in the forms of the Sphinx and centaurs, in the whole development of their art, by replacing the animal-like gods of the Asiatic world by human, indeed in Homer's presentation, all too human figures. All the fabulous beings of mixed form so abundant in Greek mythology seem to reflect again the pain and torture of this striving to be free from the mother, the result of which we admire in their sculpture of the nobly formed body freed from all earthliness and yet remaining so human.

So the deep cultural and historical importance of the development of the Greek art lies in this, that it repeats the biological and prehistorical act of becoming human, the severance from the mother and the standing upright from the earth, in the creation and perfection of its æsthetic ideal of the human body.[1] In the typical form of the gable composition, which represents a series of intermediate links—amongst them also centaurs—from the wounded warriors lying on the ground to the upright standing god, I would like to see a reflection of this biological principle of development. Moreover, the type of sitting figure (enthroned) has been dominant in the whole of Asiatic art, in so far as it copied the human being, as for example in the Buddha statues with crossed legs and in Chinese plastic art, etc. Egyptian art was the first to give prominence to the upright standing or stepping body (though still with the animal head) which in Greek art emerges as it were out of the bestial composite body as an æsthetic ideal purified from the dross of birth. In Egyptian plastic art, and in ancient Chinese rock sculpture, the figure

[1] In *Laokoön* Lessing states that among the ancients " beautiful human beings created sculpture and the state owed to the beautiful sculpture beautiful human beings."

gradually grows out of the stone ("stone birth") as, for example, the granite statue to be found in the Berlin Museum of Senmut (about 1470 B.C.) holding a princess; one sees only their heads projected from the mighty block of granite. The same *motif*, already more detached from the artistic symbol of birth, is shown by a similar group in Cairo. Hedwig Fechheimer, in her beautiful work on Egyptian plastic art,[1] states that, according to its nature, it could only accept forms remaining in complete repose as free from all objection; sitting, firmly standing, squatting, kneeling, are its most frequent motives. The granite statue of Senmut, in which the human form is completely composed in one block crowned by the head, represents in its rugged conventionality perhaps the most consistent expression of this form of spatial phantasy which borders on the architectural (pp. 25-26). From here onwards plastic art and architecture, which originally were obviously one, seem to regain their psychological connection: architecture, as "the art of space" in the true sense of the word, is a negative plastic art, just as plastic art is a "space-filling" art. "The cube figures surpass all plastic art—as do also the monumental statues by Didymaion in Miletus—in the rigid consistency of their cubistic conception. The scheme to which the complicated *position of squatting with knees drawn up high and arms folded* can be simplified is completely realized in sculpture. Both figures are completely surrounded by the cube " (p. 39).

How closely this extricating of the human being from the primal form is related by the Egyptian mind itself to the act of birth is shown in their language; " to *create* a piece of sculpture is, in Egyptian, *to bring to life*; the sculptor's

[1] In the collection *Die Kunst des Ostens*, Bd. i., Berlin.

work is designated by the causative form of the word ' to live.' That this is no mere question of assonance but of inner similarity is confirmed by the occurrence of proper names for statues, raising them to the level of individuals. . . . The myth developed the theme as follows; the primal god Ptah, who once created even himself, the gods and all things, is simultaneously the creator of art and the workshop. His High-priest bears the title " foreman of all works of art,' his name seems closely connected with a rare word for ' to form ' " (p. 13).

The double-formed Sphinx figure, which represented for the Egyptians' belief in immortality the most perfect artistic-architectural expression of rebirth, became for the Greeks the starting-point of a process of overcoming this maternal religion and thus led to the creation of the most sublime masculine ideal of art. The way in which this development advanced is easy to follow in the history of the Greek culture. Side by side with the adopted Sphinx, the Greek air is filled with phantoms which betray to us on what foundation this process of "Hellenization" rests, namely, on the most intense repression of the mother principle. Although the Sphinx, as Ilberg (see Roscher's *Lexicon*) argues, referring to Rohde and Laistner, was an adopted fabulous being, it soon became fused by the popular phantasy of the Greeks with their own products of a similar kind. These consist of the spectral army of feminine monsters which originate in very ancient beliefs and appear in such numbers only in the Greek legendary world under the form of Hecate, Gorgon, Mormo, Lamia, Gello, Empusa, under the aspect of the Keres, the Furies, Harpies, Sirens, and similar spirits of Hell and demons of death. They are all representatives of the primal mother; they portray the birth anxiety, and as such show the fundamental difference between Greek and Asiatic culture. In Asiatic culture the great primal mother enjoys godlike worship (Astarte-Kybele), whilst in Hellenism she was repressed through a reactivation of the anxiety and was replaced by a heaven of male gods, to which corresponded the man-governed state on earth.[1] Egyptian culture, from which indeed the Sphinx figure was taken over into Greece, seems to form the transition between these two extreme world views.

Egyptian culture is produced by three factors, which can all be traced back in the same way to the first effort to repress the positive attitude to the mother, which in the Asiatic world view seems to work itself out in a sexual high esteem of the primal mother, and reappears in sublimated form in the Christian mother of God. First, the *religious* factor, appearing in a peculiar cult of the dead, which in every particular detail, especially the preservation of the body, is equivalent to a further life in the womb.[2] Second, the *artistic* factor, appearing in an exaggerated esteem of the animal body (animal cult); third, the *social* factor, appearing in a high valuation of woman ("right of the mother"). These originally purely "maternal" *motifs*, in the course of a process of development lasting thousands of

[1] How incompletely this repression of the woman succeeded is shown even in the marital quarrels of Zeus, father of the gods with the mother goddess Hera; these do not lack a comical treatment even in Homer and justify the figure of the god-like " henpecked husband " which Offenbach has made of him in the gay adventurous husband. . . . The Christian counterpart to this is the devil's grandmother, who remains undisputed mistress of the underworld (p. 132). In India it is the frightful Durya.

[2] Freud has shown that the placing of the mummy in a coffin of human form indicates the return into the womb (quoted by Tausk, *l.c.*, p. 24, note).

years and making its contribution to the overcoming of the birth trauma, became masculinized, that is, remodelled in the sense of adjustment to the father libido. Typical of all three manifestations of this mother principle, as of the initial tendency to overcome it, is the veneration of the moon goddess Isis, alongside of the gradual gain in importance of her brother, son, and husband Osiris. The same is reflected in the gradual development of the *Cult of the Sun,* which not only allows assimilation with the rebirth-phantasy in Jung's sense, but in the meaning of the more original moon veneration also gives expression to the mother libido. Not only because the sun rises does the hero identify himself with it, but because it disappears every day afresh into the underworld and so corresponds to the primal wish for union with the mother=night. This is proved beyond doubt precisely by the Egyptian sun worship, with its numerous pictures that represent by preference the sun-ship on its night journey into the underworld, as also in the texts of the *Book of the Dead*: " Under the earth, thought of as a disc, another world lies, which belongs to the Departed; if the sun God meets them, the Dead raise their arms to him and praise him; the God hears the prayers of those who lie in the coffin and gives breath again to their nostrils. The ' Song of the primal Gods ' calls to the sun God, ' When you go into the underworld in the hour (?) of darkness, you wake up Osiris with your rays. When you rise over the heads of the inhabitants of the hollows (the Dead) they shout to you. . . . Let them rise who lie on their sides, when you penetrate into the underworld by night !' Special privileges enable the dead one's soul to step into the barque of the Sun and journey with him. The Dead praise the sun God with songs, which are preserved for us in the graves of the

Theban kings. . . . Because of this strong dependence of the Dead on the sun, the sun God is represented, at the end of the new Empire, in the graves; in the kings' graves the dead one meets the God as an equal " (Roscher, *Sonne*, vol. iv.).

Accordingly the very conception of the sun's origin in the Egyptian cosmology is that the sun god has begotten himself. In the song of the ancient gods, these pray: " Secret are the forms of his origin . . . who arises as Re . . . who originates from himself . . . who created himself from his own body, who bore himself; *he did not go forth from a mother's womb*; (whence) he went forth is Infinity." The other " Song of the primal Gods " says: " There is no father of him, his phallus begot him: there is no mother of him, his seed bore him. . . . Father of fathers, mother of mothers " (*l.c.*, col. 1,191). Another conception of this birth myth approaches still nearer to the embryonal primal situation, according to which the sun god created an egg, from which he himself then went forth. In the *Book of the Dead* it is written: " Re, who has risen from the ocean, says, 'I am a soul, created by the ocean. . . . My nest is not seen, my egg is not broken. . . . I have made my nest at the ends of the heavens.' " And the well-known " Illustrations of the Beetle " (mentioned by Roeder in this connection, Roscher's *Lexicon*), " which rolls a ball (that is, its egg ?) in front of it (illustration 7, *l.c.*) and indeed *into the body of the heavenly goddess, from whom it is later born*," leave no doubt that it is a matter of the primal tendency to return to the womb which also originally gave the same significance to the cult of the sun in such widely distant places of the earth as Egypt and Peru.

But the development of sun worship always goes hand in

hand with a decisive turning from mother-culture to father-culture, as is shown in the final identification of the new-born king (*infans*) with the sun. This opposition to the dominance of the woman both in the social sphere (right of the father) and in the religious, continues as the transitional process from Egypt to Greece, where it leads, by means of the entire repression of woman even from the erotic life, to the richest blossoming of the masculine civilization and to the artistic idealization corresponding to it.

THE SUN GOD IN THE LOTUS FLOWER.
(*Berlin.*)

The point of transition and also the kernel of this decisive crisis in the development of our Western civilization lies in Crete, where, as is well known, Egyptian influences first mixed with Greek, forming the Mycenean culture. This is apparent, for example, in the griffin-like figure which, according to Furtwängler, shows unmistakable agreement to the Sphinx type of the new Empire, and so also in the supposedly Egyptian Minotaur, which is formed wholly in human shape, only that the head is the head of a bull. The prison of this monster, the famous Labyrinth, has also since Weidner's important discovery become accessible to analytic understanding (verbal communication by Professor Freud). Weidner[1] has recognized from inscriptions that the inextricable, complicated dark passages of the Labyrinth are a representation of the human intestines

[1] E. F. Weidner, " Zur babylonischen Eingeweideschau. Zugleich ein Beitrag zur Geschichte des Labyrinths " (*Orient. Studien.*, Fritz Hommel zum 60 Geburtstag, I. Band, Leipzig, 1917, p. 191).

("Palace of the Intestines" it is called in the inscriptions deciphered by him). The analytic conception of these as the prison of the mis-shapen form (embryo) unable to find the exit, is clear in the sense of unconscious wish fulfilment. Whilst I reserve for a larger work[1] a detailed demonstration of this conception, the consequences of which are of immense importance for the understanding of other periods of culture (not only of the Cretan-Mycenean, but also of Northern) and of art (Labyrinth dances, Ornamentation, etc.), I would like

THE RIDERS COMING FROM THE CITY OF TROY.
(*Picture from a Pitcher from Tragliatella.*)

for the moment to set in relief the counter figure of Theseus who succeeds, by means of the thread (navel string) thrown to him by Ariadne, in finding the exit from the Labyrinth, or, according to other traditions, in freeing her from it. This, his freeing, which is represented in the phraseology of the mythical compensation as the deliverance of the chained maiden by the hero, represents the birth of the Greek ideal

[1] For the *Mikrokosmos und Makrokosmos* already mentioned. *Cf.* F. Adama van Scheltema, *Die altnordische Kunst*, Berlin, 1923, p. 115 ff.; "Der Kreis als Mutterform der Bronzezeitornamentik." Above is a sketch (according to Krause) as illustration. The representation of the famous pitcher of Tragliatella, portraying the riders coming from the Trojan fort, the "Labyrinth," in which the tail of the horse still remains in the windings (see Krause, *Die nordische Herkunft der Trojasage*, Glogau, 1893).

human being, the hero, and his detachment from the ancient primal mother.

From this point we can understand retrospectively how the near-Eastern world picture, which was a purely maternal one, led, as indicated by way of the masculinization in the Egyptian world, to the men-governed social organization of the Greeks (Sparta) and to the idealization of this purely masculine culture in the artistic creation of human beings. The most perfect expression of this course of development we find in the myth of *Prometheus*, the bold fire-bringer and creator of men, who, like his human prototype the unrivalled Greek sculptor, ventured to form men from earth and to breathe into them the fire of life.[1] This, as well as the creation of the first woman, Pandora, especially ascribed to him, places him on a level with the God of the Old Testament; only Prometheus was worshipped by the Greeks because of their need of deliverance, as friend and saviour, and his deeds were punished as titanic offences by the lord Zeus. We may expect to find again also the deepest wish fulfilment of the Unconscious in his punishment, which corresponds to his crime; he is riveted firmly to a rock standing all alone— later tradition also speaks here of " crucifixion," a bird of prey ceaselessly devours his liver, which always grows again in the night, in order to make his torture—and his unconscious pleasure—eternal.   Hence also the old tradition by

[1] As Bapp (Roscher's *Lexicon*) has already shown, it is in no way a question of the " heavenly fire " (lightning) which Prometheus steals, but of fire from the *earth* (mother).   Here links on the closely related Hephaistos-myth of the divine smith, who himself lame (birth trauma in the plunge from heaven) forms men no longer from dirty earth (*Lehm* =loam) but from noble pure metal.   See also in addition McCurdy: " Die Allmacht der Gedanken und die Mutterleibsphantasie in den Mythen von Hephästos und einem Roman von Bulwer Lytton " (*Imago*, iii., 1914).

Hesiod knows nothing of his deliverance, which only later is ascribed to Heracles, who himself represents such a hero bound eternally to a woman (Omphale), from whom he continually but vainly attempts to free himself.[1]

But the artist does the same in that he, like Prometheus, creates human beings after his own image, that is, he brings forth his work in ever new, constantly repeated acts of birth, and in it brings forth himself amid the maternal pains of creation. So the renowned artistic Greek, who understands woman only as an organ for child-bearing, and who pays homage to the love of boys, has raised himself in identification with the mother to creator of men, in that he attempts in his works of art to detach himself gradually and under great resistance from the mother, as all the Sphinx-like fabulous beings so convincingly prove. From this " moment " of simultaneously longed-for and yet not wished-for freeing from the bestial womb, from this eternal sticking fast in birth, which the neurotic constantly experi-

---

[1] *Cf.* also the later satirical conception of " Misfortune as a wife " (the unlucky box of Pandora, in which Preller recognized the *cysta mystica*, the woman's genitals) links on to the old tradition in Hesiod, according to which Zeus allows Pandora to be created on earth by Hephaistos, in order to punish Prometheus for stealing the fire. Hesiod's narrative ends with these words: " Thus Prometheus the saviour himself cannot escape the anger of Zeus, *and the mighty chains entrap him, and forcibly hold him, however cunning he is.*" That a womanly trap is meant in the deepest sense is shown by one of the oldest representations of Prometheus' punishment in a gem on one of the so-called " Island-stones " of the British Museum, which goes back again to Crete, the seat of an art " which may perhaps be called Pelasgian " (according to Roscher, iii., 2, col. 3,087).

PROMETHEUS TOR-
TURED BY AN EAGLE.

(*Stone in the British Museum.*)

ences afresh, as anxiety of the primal situation, the Greek artist and with him the entire race found the way to idealization by preserving in solid stone this stormy moment, which the Medusa head has kept in all its terrifying significance.[1]

Greek art, then, constitutes the first representation of movement. It broke up the clumsy rigidity of the Asiatic and Egyptian figures into movement, but was itself condemned again to rigidity (Lessing's *Laokoön*). The Greek, who was also the first " sportsman," has the element of movement in his physical culture, his games, his contests and dances, to the importance of which as idealized (rhythmical and composed) physical paroxysms of the unconscious (spasms, attacks) we can here only refer in passing.[2]

After all, we may have to look for the beginning of every art in general in plastic art. But before primitive man started like Prometheus, to form men in clay, presumably, on the analogy of the instinct of nest-building, he first created a vessel for a receptacle and a protection, in imitation of the womb.[3] The ancient Babylonian tradition of

[1] The process of idealization can be followed in the transition from the horrifying Gorgonic gorge, to the Medusa Rondanini, the Greek Madonna (see the corresponding illustration in Roscher, i., 2, col. 1716-17, 1723). *Cf.* Ferenczi, " Zur Symbolik des Medusenhauptes " (*Int. Zschr. f. Ps.A.*, ix., 1, 1923, p. 69) and the supplementary remark of Freud's, " The Infantile Genital Organization of the Libido," *Coll. Papers*, vol. ii., p. 247, note 2.

[2] *Cf.* the description and history of the " Labyrinth dances " by Krause. In the Roman circus games which still survive in our racecourse, the race, going round and round, takes place as if in labyrinthine passages.

[3] Fuhrmann (*Der Sinn im Gegenstand*, p. 2 f.) distinguishes two types of vessels: those not made for liquids are formed after the shape of the animal intestines, from which the roll-shaped technique of the ceramic art developed (*i.e.*, in New Guinea). " The belly-

the god who makes men on the potter's wheel—as the god Chnum is represented in the temple of Luxor—points in the same direction. The original vessel, as in the "Myth of the Birth of the Hero," is the womb, which it first imitates. Soon the vessel undergoes a still clearer development in the direction of representing the original content, namely, the diminutive human being, the child, or its *head* (*Kopf, Topf,* pot). It gets a belly, ears, a beak, etc. (*cf.* the typical head-beakers, for example, of the primitives, the urns with faces, etc.[1] This early human creation, therefore, faithfully repeats the biological development from vessel to (the therein found) child. And when the later real art, which, so to say, completely freed human beings from the vessel, produced completed human beings, as did Prometheus and the Greek sculptors, we have to recognize in it the tendency to avoid the birth trauma, the painful deliverance.

In this we perceive the real root of art, namely, in this

---

shaped pot faithfully represents in its foundation the lower body of man, thus an endless line of spirally arranged intestines, which are clothed outwardly by a skin and contain the stomach inside, or receive the stock of nourishment. . . . Those made for liquids are formed like the udder of the animal or like the breast of a woman (see *Schlauch =outre =uterus; Bocksbeutel, Beutel =bouteille =bottle*), so that every bottle is an udder, that stands on its base " the teat upwards."

[1] The later decoration *on* the vessel replaces the original *content in* the vessel, as the Peruvian ceramic shows with particular clearness (see in Fuhrmann's *Peru,* i., especially the remarkable animal and human figures on the bellied, body-shaped vessels of the Chimu culture, illustration 6 ff.). Similarly also the ornamentation on the famous pitcher of Tragliatella is to be understood as the representation on the surface of what is inside. . . . In the Hindu Bhagavad Gita bodies are called *Kscheta,* that is, *vessels,* fruit-bearing ground, womb (according to Winterstein, *l.c.,* p. 8).

autoplastic imitation[1] of one's own growing and origin from the maternal vessel; for the copying of this vessel itself might have been made subservient to practical needs, whilst the formation according to one's own body signifies the achievement characteristic of art, of apparent purpose-lessness which is yet somehow full of meaning. In this sense art developed, so to say, as a branch of "applied art," which indeed it was originally, and as such it plays a quite important part in real culture. Moreover, it is certainly no accident that the Greeks, idealizing above everything the masculine body, should have attained in the composition and refinement of the maternal vessel the highest stage of perfection in their vases.

In the naturalistic animal representations of the Ice Age we have before us the corresponding beginnings of painting. In these cave-drawings man seems to have reproduced the animal body as a symbol to him of the warmth-giving shelter, the cave. Only thus is it intelligible, why "single animals or groups of animals in deep places in chapels and niches, are accessible only after overcoming considerable and difficult obstacles (which can bring the ignorant in danger of life) often only by creeping on hands and knees" (Schneider, l.c., p. 5).[2] This conception would not only not contradict the prevailing "magical" explanation, but would make it psychologically (from the unconscious) intelligible: it is still a question of animals, which warm,

[1] Verworn has inferred the character of prehistoric art, called by him "physioplastic," from the perfection and lack of development of diluvial naturalism (*Zur Psychologie der primitiven Kunst*, 1908). Reinach has coined the aptly ambiguous phrase for it: "Proles sine matre creata, mater sine prole defuncta" (according to Scheltema, *l.c.*, p. 8).

[2] See R. Schmidt, *Die Kunst der Eiszeit*, 1922, and Herb. Kühn, *Die Malerei der Eiszeit*, 1922.

protect, and nourish human beings, as once the mother did.

In the later painting, for example, in Christian art, the whole life of Jesus from His birth to His death is pictorially represented to people ignorant of reading, so that identification easily becomes possible. Mary with the child finally develops in Italian art as the symbol of the blessedness of motherhood, that is, of the blessedness of child and mother in union. So the individual redeemer dissolves again into the separate divine individuals, the children. The crucified and " reborn " Christ is here pictured as an ordinary child at the mother's breast.

The modern art movements which betray so many primitive characteristics would then be the last projections of the " psychologizing " art school which consciously represents " the interior " of man, namely, his unconscious, and predominantly in " embryonal " forms.[1]

We have now come to the very root of the problem of art, which is finally a *problem of form*. As it appears to us, all " form " goes back to the primal form of the maternal vessel, which has become to a large extent the content of art; and indeed in an idealized and sublimated way, namely, as form, which makes the primal form, fallen under repression, again acceptable, in that it can be represented and felt as " beautiful."

If now we ask how it was possible for the Greek people to bring about such an extensive idealization of the birth trauma, ancient Greek history may give us a hint for the understanding of this remarkable development. I am

[1] See Hermann Bahr, *Expressionismus*, 1916, Oskar Pfister, *Der psychol. ü. biolog. Untergrund d. Expressionismus*, 1920, and finally Prinzhorn, *Die Bildnerei der Geisteskranken*, 1922.

thinking of the Doric migration, which drove out a part of the Greek people in early times from their native land and compelled them to look for a new motherland on the Ionian Islands lying opposite and on the coast of Asia Minor. This compulsory separation from the native land seems, in the sense of a repetition of the birth trauma, the violent severance from the mother, to have determined the entire further development of Greek culture. It seems quite certain that the Homeric epics, especially the *Iliad*, represent the first artistic reaction to the conclusion of this great migration of people, this colonization of the coast of Asia Minor by the Greek settlers. The battle for the Trojan fortress, and the eternally youthful Helen, abducted thither from her native land, reflects again the desperate attempts of the Greek emigrants to establish themselves in a new land; whereas the Homeric battles of the gods seem to indicate a repetition of the battle of the laboriously set-up Olympic dominance of Zeus against the cult of the mother idol (Athene), still prevailing in Asia Minor. I hope sometime to be able to show from the analysis of the content of epic phantasies how real historical truths can be peeled off from the luxuriant growths of unconscious elaboration, and thus how ancient Greek history can be reconstructed. Professor Freud proposed this to me many years ago, urging me to trace the psychoanalytically recognized mechanism of epic formation in the Homeric poems.[1] For the present I should like only to emphasize the fact that the Greek cult of Demeter (Γή-μήτηρ =Mother earth) related to the Asiatic

[1] See my preparations for this (*Imago*, v., 1917-19), " Psychologische Beiträge zur Entstehung des Volksepos I Homer " (Das Problem), II, " Die Dichterische Phantasiebildung " (where, p. 137, note, will be found a sketch of the work, which hitherto has not gone beyond the stage of preparation).

mother goddesses, was, according to Herodotus, established on the Peloponnesian Isles before the Dorian immigration. This supports our assumption that the population driven forth by the Dorian invaders was firmly fixed on the mother earth, whilst, on the other hand, it may perhaps indicate that the Dorians took refuge in the love of boys as a reaction to this all too maternal attachment. The figure of Heracles, according to Wilamowitz a faithful reflection of the valiant nobility of the Peloponnesian Dorians, would then have preserved, in the sense of making heroic, the difficulties of this severance from the mother. For Heracles appears also in pre-Homeric tradition as conqueror of Troy.

The Homeric representation gives us a good example of how the poet, in attempting to remember painful historical events, sinks back to his own unconscious wish phantasies. Whilst the *Iliad* describes only the unavailing battles for Troy, in the Odyssey, the famous conclusion of this *ten years'* contest is narrated retrospectively. The cunning hero brings the contests to an end in the famous history of the wooden horse, in whose belly the hidden Achæan heroes reach the innermost fortress. This human and at the same time deeply poetic tradition clearly shows that the emigrants,[1] violently driven from their native land, had as their final goal the regaining of the eternally young and

[1] Similarly as regards the expulsion of the Israelites from Egypt, this most important traumatic event in their history, from which their entire further fate follows and which corresponds exactly to the primal trauma of the expulsion from Paradise. Since that time the Jews seek this promised land where *milk* and honey flow, without being able to find it (Ahasuerus). Moreover, the expulsion from Paradise, on account of enjoyment of the forbidden fruit (mother's breast), reflects the strict necessity of the weaning trauma, which man by means of adjustment to reality seeks to compensate by the winning of artificial nourishment from the earth (agriculture).

beautiful maternal ideal (Helena)[1] from a strange land. And the only possible form of fulfilment for the Unconscious was the return into the animal-like womb, which would be unworthy as a refuge and protection for fearless heroes did we not know that their heroic nature itself springs from the difficulty of the birth trauma and the compensation of fear. So the Trojan horse is the direct unconscious counterpart to the native Centaurs and Sphinxes, which creations were later to initiate and carry out the sublime process of freeing from the mother. But also Troy itself, the impregnable, the innermost part of which one can reach only through cunning, is like every fortress a symbol of the mother.[2] Thus is explained the *signification of the underworld* which mythologists assign to Troy, and even its close relationship with the Cretan and northern Labyrinths, which Ernst Krause (Carus Sterne) has established[3] beyond any doubt in a brilliant book, marred only by too much historico-mythological thought.

The proverbial cunning of Odysseus, which, moreover, is appropriate to all " celestial hotspurs " of Greek mythology and brings them to their downfall into Tartaros (underworld) and to eternal punishment, throws an important

[1] As is well known, it is told that, before taking possession of the town, the protecting statue of Athene had been carried off by Odysseus and Diomedes from an Adytum placed under the cella of the goddess, through subterranean canals or brook ravines.

[2] See my treatise, " Um Städte werben," *Int. Zschr. f. Ps.A.*, i., 1913.

[3] *Die Trojaburgen Nordeuropas*. Ihr Zusammenhang mit der indogermanischen Trojasage von der entführten und gefangenen Sonnenfrau, den Trojaspielen, Schwert- und Labyrinthtänzen zur Feier ihrer Lenzbefreiung. With twenty-six illustrations in the text. Glogau, 1893.

light on the psychology of the poet.[1] Odysseus, the narrator of all these false fairy tales which tell of the return to the womb, quite obviously represents the poet himself, and may, moreover, be considered the representative and primal father of all epic poets, whose function seems to be to depreciate the primal trauma through fictitious exaggeration, and thereby still maintain the illusion of a primal reality lying behind the primal phantasy. Yet the latest followers of this kind of story-telling, as, for example, the now famous Baron von Münchausen, try to represent the impossible, the unattainable—even that directly contradicting Nature, as, for instance, to draw oneself out of the water by the hair— as the easiest thing in the world, so that the very impossibility of the situation represents for the Unconscious the most calming and gratifying element.[2]

In contrast to this artful breaker of natural and divine laws who yet somehow enables this constantly unfulfilled wish to be gratified in the fictitious narratives, stands the typical *simpleton* who in a remarkable way performs the most impossible tasks in play. But his stupidity is nothing

[1] I have touched on the psychological relationship of the poet to the hero in my study on " Die Don Juan-Gestalt," *Imago*, viii., 1922, p. 193.

[2] The *unnatural* often proves to be connected with the non-realization of the womb situation and its representation. So in Macbeth, the threat that he will fall when the Birnam wood moves on him (instead of his going into the wood); this warning corresponds to the others that only an unborn, namely, Macduff, cut out of his mother's body, will conquer him (*cf.* also the head of the unborn child which appears to Macbeth and the bloody head). From this cardinal point of the play, which according to Freud rests on the theme of childlessness, much that is enigmatical becomes intelligible. One may compare with this Freud's remarks about " the uncanny " (*Imago*, v., 1917-19) in poetry, which finally also corresponds to the womb situation (*l.c.*, p. 261 ff.).

but an expression of his infantilism; he is also an *infans*, as inexperienced as the new-born god Horus, who is represented with his finger in his mouth. The more stupid and therefore the more childlike he is, the sooner will he succeed in the fulfilment of the primal wish, and if, like little *Tom Thumb* of the fairy tales, he has only the stature of the first embryonal phase, then he is almost omnipotent and has attained the ideal state of which the neurotic still so often dreams,[1] and which the new-born mythical heroes seem to represent, namely, that of being quite small again, and yet participator in all the advantages of a grown-up person.[2]

On the other hand, tragedy (which likewise was brought to the highest perfection by the Greeks, and which according to Nietzsche perished in " æsthetic Socratism," that is, in the hypertrophy of consciousness) grew up from the mimic representations of the mythical rites, and symbolized the sufferings and punishments of the mythical hero[3] on account of his " tragic guilt." This has become known to us in its unconscious significance from the analysis of mythical tradition, and the origin of tragedy from the dances and songs of the participators in the sacrifice who were enveloped in goat skin shows clearly what was involved. The skin in which the participators envelop themselves after the sacrifice and disembowelment of the animal is again nothing but a substitute for the protecting womb. This partial realization of the return to the mother has likewise found a lasting

---

[1] *Cf.* the expression of one of Freud's patients (*Interpretation of Dreams*) who regretted not having made better use of his nurse's breast when a child.

[2] Ferenczi first drew attention to this " dream of the wise suckling " (*Int. Zschr. f. Ps.A.*, ix., p. 70).

[3] *Cf.* also Winterstein, " Zur Entstehungsgeschichte der griechischen Tragödie," *Imago*, viii., 1922.

pictorial expression in the numerous goat-legged and goat-headed fauns and satyrs of Greek mythology[1] and sculpture. In the art of tragedy which, like the dance, takes the living human being itself as its object, the frightful and primitive character of the repressed primal wish lives on in a milder form as tragic guilt, which every individual mortal spectator can re-enact by continuously re-experiencing it: whereas in epic poetry we see the attempts to overcome the primal wish by fictitious transformations. The highest idealization of the birth trauma attained in plastic art is, in compassion-arousing tragedy, resolved once again into the malleable primal element of the anxiety affect, capable of outlet, whereas in epic and satiric poetry the too highly strung idealization breaks out as boastful untruthfulness.

Art, as a representation and at the same time denial of reality, thus resembles the childish game in which we have recognized the attempt to depreciate the primal trauma through the consciousness of not being serious. From here the way leads to the understanding of humour; this highest stage in the overcoming of repression is achieved by a quite definite attitude of the Ego to its own Unconscious. But we cannot here trace the origin of humour, for it would lead us again deeply into the theory of neurosis and its therapy based on the psychology of the Ego.

---

[1] In a thoroughgoing psychoanalytic investigation, " Panik und Pan-Komplex " (*Imago*, vi., 1920), Dr. B. Felszeghy has traced the affect of "panic" fright, in connection with Ferenczi's investigations concerning the development of the sense of Reality, back to the repetition of the birth anxiety, and has made the remarkable mythical form of Pan completely intelligible from this significance. Much already finds expression in Felszeghy, which in our work gains fresh illumination from another side.

PHILOSOPHIC SPECULATION

GREEK philosophy, which is really the first to deserve the name, and which was later linked with physics—although Aristotle was right in designating his predecessors as near relatives of Philomythos—shows in its origin among the Ionian Nature philosophers the naïve counterpart to the idealizing tendency which was stretched to its utmost in Greek art and mythology. These early Western thinkers from Thales to Socrates seem to form the transitional stage between the cosmic world view of the ancient East and our natural scientific point of view, and are, therefore, the forerunners of our present-day Western European mentality.

Whilst the Oriental world view attempted by a sublime cosmic projection to derive earthly destiny from the cosmic celestial-image,[1] the Ionian thinkers accomplished the separation of these spheres in an unsophisticated view, and in going back to the original mother, Nature, they attempted to conceive earthly life as freed from supernatural influence. That this could only succeed because the Greeks simultaneously banished the entire Oriental mythology of the heavens into the underworld, in the real sense of the word, we have already mentioned in the previous chapter. Through this purification of the air from cosmological phantasies, they were in the position to see and to com-

[1] Among the Babylonians astrology goes parallel with augury applied to the intestines of the sacrificial animal. The human being and his inward parts were projected to the heavens (see my *Mikrokosmos und Makrokosmus*, now in preparation).

prehend natural laws in their simple form, just where the Oriental world view recognized only heavenly laws which worked themselves out on earth.

Greek philosophy begins, as is well known, with Thales's statement that *water* is the origin and womb of all things.[1] Before following the further development of Greek thought from this concentrated formula,[2] let us make clear to ourselves that with this statement the first dim conception of the individual origin of Man in the mother is extended to a universal natural law. The mechanism of this cognition, which is doubtless right biologically,[3] is distinguished from the cosmic and mythical projection of the heavenly waters (milky way) and the rivers of the underworld (stream of the dead) by the fact that this is a real discovery, the drawing away of a curtain, or, as we should say, the removal of a repression, which had hitherto prevented the discovery of the origin of all life in water, just because man himself had once come out of the amniotic fluid. The prerequisite for the discovery of a truth is therefore the recognition of the Unconscious in the outer world by the removal of an inner repression, which starts directly—as the development of philosophy clearly shows—from the primal repression.

Thales's successor, Anaximander of Miletus, the first philosophic author of the ancients, already shows a reaction to this, when he says: "Whence things originated, thither,

[1] *Cf.* " Die Bedeutung des Wassers im Kult und Leben der Alten. Eine symbolgeschichtliche Untersuchung," by Martin Ninck (*Philologue Suppl.*, Bd. xiv., Heft 2, Leipzig, 1921).

[2] According to Nietzsche, *Die Philosophie im tragischen Zeitalter der Griechen* (" Philosophy during the Tragic Age of the Greeks," *Early Greek Philosophy*) (1873), from which all following quotations are taken. *Works*, edited Levy, p. 73 ff.

[3] In addition, now see Ferenczi's phylogenetic parallel to individual development (*Versuch einer Genitaltheorie*, 1924).

according to necessity, they must return and perish; for they must pay penalty and be judged for their injustices according to the order of time."[1] Nietzsche rightly interprets this oracular expression as the first pessimistic note of philosophy, and compares it with an utterance of the classical pessimist Schopenhauer, whose whole attitude to life and to the world is thus explained: " The right standard by which to judge every human being is that he really is a being who ought not to exist at all, but who is expiating his existence by manifold forms of suffering and death: What can one expect from such a being ? Are we not all sinners condemned to death ? We expiate our birth firstly by our life and secondly by our death."[2] Anaximander's statement thus supplements Thales's knowledge by emphasizing the return to the very origin of all, and reveals through psychological intuition a second law of Nature which was taken over only in somewhat changed form into our scientific thought.[3]

[1] Nietzsche, " Philosophy during the Tragic Age of the Greeks," *Early Greek Philosophy*, p. 92.

[2] *Ibid.*, pp. 92-93.

[3] Who knows whether Nietzsche's casual anthropomorphic " idea " that " all inorganic material has arisen from organic; it is dead organic material, corpse and man " will not sometime " revalue " natural science. S. Rado has recently attempted to show how far also the exact natural sciences are unconsciously determined: " Die Wege der Naturforschung im Lichte der Psychoanalyse " (*Imago*, viii., 1922). For the first steps in chemistry, alchemy, Jung has already coined the comprehensive formula that it sets out ultimately to beget children without a mother (*cf.* H. Silberer's " Der Homunkulus," *Imago*, iii., 1914, and *Probleme der Mystik und ihrer Symbolik*, 1914). One should read in connection with modern chemistry the interesting article by Dr. Alfred Robitsek: " Symbolisches Denken in der chemischen Forschung " (*Imago*, i., 1912). It is, moreover, psychologically remarkable that the actual destroyer of alchemy and the first natural scientific chemist, Justus Liebig, was the inventor of artificial manure and of meat extract and so fulfilled the alchemistic wish-dream in a symbolically realistic manner.

By showing how, from the transience of all earthly things, the Greek thinker comes to the necessary assumption of an "indefinite" one, a primal being, the womb of all things, Nietzsche succeeds in giving us a glimpse into the way which leads from there beyond the platonic "idea" to the Kantian "thing-in-itself," in which Schopenhauer was the first to recognize the "will" once again, although still in philosophic disguise. From this conflict between origin and disappearance, arising directly from the repression of the primal trauma, Heraclitus tried to save himself by his law of eternal becoming, in that he recognized, quite in the sense of the primal repression, "the proper course of all becoming and passing which he conceived of under the form of polarity, as the divergence *of one* force into two qualitatively different opposite actions striving after reunion."[1] If what is meant here is the primal ambivalence connected with the act of becoming (birth), then the qualitative substratum of this state is not lacking. Anaximander had already developed the theory of (cold) water by stating that it originated from "warmth" and "dampness" as its primary stage, and the "physicist" Heraclitus then reinterpreted "this Anaximandrian 'warmth' as the respiration, the warm breath, the dry vapours, in short, as the fiery element; about this fire he now enunciates what Thales and Anaximander had enunciated about water: that in innumerable metamorphoses it was passing along the path of Becoming, especially in the three chief aggregate stages as something Warm, Moist, or Firm."[2] In this way Heraclitus discovered atmospheric circulation with its periodicity, which, in contrast to Anaximander, he conceives, in the sense that the

[1] Nietzsche, "Philosophy during the Tragic Age of the Greeks," *Early Greek Philosophy*, p. 101.
[2] *Ibid.*, p. 105.

constantly renewed extinction in the all-destroying universal conflagration " is characterized as a demand and a need; the state of being completely swallowed up by the fire as satiety."[1] With this knowledge of the pleasurable return into nothingness, which again seems to make the becoming an insoluble problem, simple contemplation freed from repression turns once more to speculation under the influence of a new wave of repression.

Whilst Heraclitus could rightly say, " I sought and investigated myself," his successor Parmenides, turning away from this close contemplation of realities, launches forth into the logical abstractions of " being " and " not being." He spun these out of the originally quite real and human facts of being and not being, which in their anthropomorphic application to the world can yet be traced linguistically; for " *esse* means at the bottom: ' to breathe !' " (Nietzsche). By logical deduction Parmenides then arrived at the first criticism of our instrument of knowledge through which we can only recognize appearances, and thus prepared the way for that philosophical separation of "mind and body " which still continues to exist in our scientific thought. Here an attempt is made for the first time to establish logically the idealistic world view, which in Plato, and still more clearly in his Hindu forerunners, started from a withdrawal by mystical meditation into the primal condition.

Anaxagoras then took a further step in natural science and in the theory of knowledge by disputing the possibility that, from the one primal element, the womb of Becoming, a plurality of qualities could proceed. According to him, there are from the beginning numerous substances which

[1] *Ibid.*, p. 105.

only through movement produce the variety and multiplicity of the world. "That Motion, however, is a truth and not Appearance Anaxagoras proved in opposition to Parmenides by the indisputable succession of our conceptions in thinking." But now in order to explain the movement of ideas, he assumed in "mind in itself," in *Nous*, "a *first* moment of motion in some primeval age, as the *Chalaza* of all so-called Becoming; that is, of all Change."[1] And so finally by the roundabout way of logical deduction he reached that now famous primal state, Chaos, in which *Nous* had not yet operated on material, and was therefore still unmoved, resting in a blessed mixed state, which Anaxagoras described by the expression "seed of all things." The way in which this thinker pictures to himself the formation of the Cosmos, from out this chaos of the circle moved by the *Nous*, approaches, despite all its primitive representations of the human procreation (as already shown by Nietzsche), the laws of mechanics, which two thousand years later Kant was to proclaim in his inspiring pronouncements on the natural history of the heavens.

The early Greek philosophers could not, therefore, get away from the primal problem of Becoming, from the question of the origin of things. They wandered along different ways, followed by the later philosophers, and withdrawing ever further and further from the real problem of the origin of man, which lay behind the primal repression. It was reserved for the genius of Plato to reverse the problem in his doctrine of Eros, and so also in the field of philosophy to rediscover the human being as the measure of all things, as almost simultaneously Greek art had discovered it.

[1] *Ibid.*, p. 145.

Plato's philosophy of Eros, which has already been fully appreciated from the psychoanalytic side,[1] places the human instinct of procreation at the centre of things, and points in its world explanation to the different stages of Eros, as shown in the sensuous, the psychical, the philosophic, and the religious (mystical) attitude. Here for the first time the philosophical problem is grasped at the root, and we ought therefore not to be surprised if Plato uses for the presentation of his doctrine similes which come very close to the biological facts. He conceives Eros as the yearning for a lost state, indeed still more clearly, for a lost union, and he also explains the essence of the sexual impulse in his famous allegory of the primal being cut in two, as a striving towards reunion. This is the clearest conscious approach to the desire for reunion of the child with the mother which had hitherto been attained in the history of the human mind, and with which Freud was able to relate his libido theory.[2] Indeed, Plato, in harmony with the Orphic-dionysiæ religion, approaches most nearly to ultimate biological knowledge when he says: " Eros is the *Pain wherewith the Demon, who through his own enigmatic guilt was plunged into birth,*[3] *reclaims the lost Paradise of his pure and original Being."*

But because Plato through some extraordinary intuition felt this intense longing within himself and represented it,

[1] Especially in Winterstein's valuable investigation, " Psychoanalytische Anmerkungen zur Geschichte der Philosophie " (*Imago*, ii., 1913). Later by Nachmannsohn, "Freud's Libidotheorie verglichen mit der Eroslehre Platos " (*Int. Zschr. f. Ps.A.*, iii., 1915) and Pfister's " Plato als Vorläufer der Psychoanalyse " (*ibid.*, vii., 1921).

[2] Freud, *Jenseits des Lustprinzips*, 1921.

[3] " The expression ' plunge ' in birth is found not only among the Orphics, but also in Buddhism " (Winterstein, *l.c.*, p. 184).

he now projects it, in conformity with the inexorable primal repression, to the whole outer world, and so succeeds in recognizing in all things the yearning for the transcendental, the striving for perfection, the will to ascend to the primal image of the " Idea." How near psychologically this concept is to that of origin from a primal being does not require elucidation[1] from the primitive thoughts of other peoples, because its unconscious significance is so clear. Platonic idealism as it appears in this concept, the break with the physical world, with which Plato obviously has to pay for his insight into the inner world, finds in the famous comparison of human existence with a subterranean cave, on whose walls one perceives only the shadows of real processes, a wish-fulfilling representation, which throws a clear light on the subjective source of Plato's insight. The comparison to the cave is not merely " a womb phantasy," as Winterstein (l.c.) has already supposed, but it gives us a deep glimpse into the mind of the philosopher, who experienced Eros driving everything onwards as a yearning for the return into the primal state, and at the same time created the expression of the highest philosophic sublimation for it in his doctrine of ideas.[2]

If man's philosophical cognition reached its climax in Plato, it now remains to explain what compelled the thinkers of the following two thousand years to turn aside from this sublime synthesis and idealization of early Greek philoso-phical development and to pursue the stony path of repres-

[1] Winterstein (l.c., p. 193).

[2] The phylogenetic supplement to this, according to Nietzsche's thought, is Pythagoras' transmigration of souls, which answers the question how we can know anything about ideas: by remembering an earlier existence; but biologically expressed, this can only mean the embryonic state.

sion and intellectual displacement.   Plato had come so near
to the sought-for primal knowledge that a strong reaction
was unavoidable, and we recognize in Aristotle, his immediate
pupil and successor, the bearer of this reaction.   By deviating
from the philosophically formulated primal trauma Aristotle
succeeded in making a natural scientific conquest of a new
part of reality, whereby he became the father of all the
natural and mental sciences.   But for this he had again to
close his eyes to the urge within, and by an obsessional
neurotic displacement of the repressed primal libido on to the
processes of thought, to bring into rich bloom the logical
and dialectical speculation on which the whole of Western
philosophy was nourished up to the time of Schopenhauer, who was the first to revert to the Hindu primal
wisdom and its philosophic expression in Plato.   It would
lead us too far even to trace in outline the development
of Aristotelian thought, which exercised so enormous an
influence on the intellectual history of Europe, just because
it led mankind ever deeper into scholastic speculation
and thus apparently ever further away from repression.   I
say apparently, for even in the most logical abstractions of
the Aristotelians, there are such tangible traces[1] of the
primal repression that these alone would suffice to explain
the continued tendency to speculation.   On the other hand,
the generally introverted intellectual tendency of the
speculative logician and of the mystic psychologically akin
to him, shows that, with the intellectual removal of repression, his whole psychical attitude approaches ever closer

[1] In a work submitted to the editorial staff of *Imago* by
E. Roeder, " Das Ding an sich," this is shown in detail even for the
biological thing in itself, the embryo in the womb, from which
idea especially the entire (geometric) space concept of Aristotle is
deduced.

to the primal situation of meditation and abandonment which he tries to avoid in the content of his thought.

The philosophical mystics thus represent the direct continuation of religious mysticism, which consists in sinking into one's own inner meditation. They call the God, whom they now look for in their own inner being, Knowledge, but the aim is the same: the *unio mystica*, the being at one with the All. That this mystical experience is strongly coloured sexually, that the union with the godhead is felt and experienced under the likeness of a sexual union[1] (to know= *coire*), is shown by the libidinal foundation for this fundamental striving, the return into the primal state. It is written in the Upanishads: "Just as when a man is embraced by the beloved, he has *no consciousness* of that which is *outside and inside*, so also the mind which is engulfed by the primal self, has no consciousness of that which is outside or inside." And Plotinus says of the mystical ecstasy: "There is no intervening space there, there are no longer two, but *both are one*, they are not separate one from another, so long as that one is there. *This union is imitated here in this world by lover and the beloved*, who desire to fuse with one another into one being."[2] As already the Hindu *tat twam*

[1] See Pfister, *Hysterie und Mystik bei Margareta Ebner* (1291-1351), 1910 (*Zum Kampf um die Psychoanalyse*, chap. v., 1920); *Die Frömmigkeit des Grafen Ludwig von Zinzendorf. Ein psa. Beitrag z. Kenntnis der relig. Sublimierungsprozesse und zur Erklärung des Pietismus*, 1910. Further, A. Kielholz, *Jakob Boehme. Ein pathographischer Beitrag zur Psychologie der Mystik*, 1919. See also G. Hahn, *Die Probleme der Hysterie und die Offenbarungen der Heiligen Therese*, 1906.

[2] Plotinus himself suffered from such ecstatic, visionary soul-raptures, as he reports in the *Enneads* (iv., 8, 1). This freeing of the soul from the compulsion of fatal necessity and of rebirth is taught also by theurgists, magicians, and Gnostics. Genuine theurgists, such as the Neo-Platonists, attained this in themselves by

asi (you yourself are that) shows, it is a question of doing away with the boundaries between the Ego and the non-Ego; in prayer, this is attempted by becoming one with God (with this compare the verse of Mechthild: "I am in you and you are in me," Heiler, *Das Gebet*). And an Islamic mystic cries out in blessed ecstasy: "The Ego and the You have ceased to exist between us, I am not I, You are not You, also You are not I; I am at the same time I and You, You are at the same time You and I. I am confused whether You are I or I You " (*l.c.*).

As we have seen, the neo-Platonists and their successors completely succeeded, though certainly at the cost of philosophical insight, in realizing that striving for union with their origin which was so poetically formulated in their Founder's philosophy of Eros. As a reaction to it appears modern philosophy, which, like Greek philosophy, took its point of departure from the discovery of man as a part of Nature and sought intellectually to deny and to abolish his separation from it. This begins on a higher psychical stage of development with Descartes' *discovery of the Ego*, as something distinct from the non-Ego, in order finally to culminate in the ingenious expansion of the Ego in the Kantian system, whilst the hypertrophic Ego systems, such as Fichte's, represent the counterpart to the mythological projection of the Ego into the surrounding world. But even Kant only succeeded in recognizing and conceiving as a theory of knowledge the apriority of the ideas of space and time as *inborn* categories from the immediateness of the

---

meditating and pondering in detail over ultimate things and also by physical preparation, such as continuous fasting and self-castigation of all kinds (see Th. Hopfner, " Über die Geheimlehren von Jamblichus," *Quellenschr. d. Griech. Mystik.*, Bd. I., Leipzig, 1922).

intrauterine state, in that he gratified the transcendental tendencies of his Unconscious on the one hand through the sublime compensation of his knowledge of cosmic laws, and on the other hand through his pathologically eccentric existence. The " thing-in-itself," which he allowed as the only transcendental, and therefore impenetrable, reality, naturally escaped him.

Not merely does this development of philosophical thought betray to us that this " thing-in-itself " is again identical with the mysterious, strongly repressed primal foundation of our being, the mother's womb, but Schopenhauer's further philosophical modification of this concept through the " will " again humanizes the " thing-in-itself " and transfers it to our inner self, where Nietzsche claims to see it as the egoistic will to power, whilst Psychoanalysis by its new-found paths to " self-knowledge " has made it psychologically comprehensible as the unconsciously working primal libido.

This " know thyself," which Psychoanalysis first really took seriously, leads us back to Socrates, who took this command of the Delphic Apollo as the foundation of his doctrine. Up till now we have not spoken of this direct predecessor of Plato, without whom Plato himself and all who came after him are psychologically inconceivable. For before the picture of Socrates going consciously and fearlessly to his death his friend and pupil Plato, as Nietzsche says, " threw himself down in fervent and enthusiastic devotion," and dedicated his life to the fostering and preservation of his master's memory. But Socrates' philosophy only shows the concrete substratum of the primal trauma, to which his pupil Plato and his successor Aristotle have reacted in such far-reaching ways. With the appearance of Socrates, who is distinguished as a special type among the philosophers before and after him, that decisive turning towards the inner self enters into Greek thought which preserves its philosophic formation through Plato and is already characterized by the fact that Socrates, as Xenophon reports in his *Memorabilia*, expressly rejects as useless meditation about the origin of the world and the questions related to it.

In order to be able fully to appreciate the importance of Socrates, in whom Nietzsche sees " the turning point and crown of so-called world history," we must go back again to Nietzsche's penetrating psychoanalysis of this his arch-adversary in the *Birth of Tragedy*. " ' Only by instinct ': with this phrase we touch upon the heart and core of the Socratic tendency.   Socratism condemns therewith existing art as well as existing ethics. . . . From this point onwards Socrates believed that he was called upon to correct existence; and, with an air of disregard and superiority, as the precursor of an altogether different culture, art and morality, he enters single-handed into the world. . . . Here is the extraordinary hesitancy which always seizes upon us with regard to Socrates, and again and again invites us to ascertain the sense and purpose of this most questionable phenomenon of antiquity.   Who is it that ventures single-handed to disown the Greek character ?[1]"

" A key to the character of Socrates is presented to us by the surprising phenomenon designated as the ' daimonion ' of Socrates.   In special circumstances, when his gigantic intellect began to stagger, he got a secure support in the utterances of a divine voice which then spoke to him. This voice, whenever it comes, always *dissuades*.   In this

---

[1] Nietzsche, *Birth of Tragedy*, pp. 103-4.   (*Works*, edited by Dr. Oscar Levy.)

totally abnormal nature instinctive wisdom only appears
in order to hinder the progress of conscious perception here
and there.   While in all productive men it is instinct which
is the creatively affirmative force, consciousness only com-
porting itself critically and dissuasively, in Socrates it is
instinct which becomes critic, it is consciousness which
becomes creator—a perfect monstrosity *per defectum.*"[1]

To this diagnosis Nietzsche almost twenty years later
added an analysis of the man Socrates, which in its inexor-
ableness not only does not pause before the all too human,
but applies itself just to that: " To judge from his origin,
Socrates belonged to the lowest of the low: Socrates was
mob.   You know, and you can still see it for yourself, how
ugly he was.   But ugliness, which in itself is an objection,
was almost a refutation among the Greeks.   Was Socrates
really a Greek ?   Ugliness is not infrequently the expression
of thwarted development, or of development arrested by
crossing.   In other cases, it appears as a decadent development.   The anthropologists among the criminal specialists
declare that the typical criminal is ugly; *monstrum in fronte,*
monstrum in animo. . . .   Not only are the acknowledged
wildness and anarchy of Socrates' instincts indicative of
decadence, but also that preponderance of the logical facul-
ties and that malignity of the mis-shapen which was his
special characteristic.   Neither should we forget those
aural delusions which were religiously interpreted as ' the
demon of Socrates.' "[2]

" On the occasion when that physiognomist had unmasked
Socrates, and had told him what he was—a crater full of evil

[1] Nietzsche, *Birth of Tragedy,* pp. 104-105.   Translated works
edited by O. Levy.
[2] " The Problem of Socrates," *The Twilight of the Idols (Götzendäm-*
merung, 1888), p. 11, vol. xvi., translated works.

desires—the great Master of Irony let fall one or two words more which provide the key to his nature. ' This is true,' he said, ' but I overcame them all.' How did Socrates succeed in mastering himself ? His case was at bottom only the extreme and most apparent example of a state of distress which was beginning to be general; that state in which no one was able to master himself and in which the instincts turned one against the other. As the extreme example of this state, he fascinated—his terrifying ugliness made him conspicuous to every eye; it is quite obvious that he fascinated still more as a reply, as a solution, as an apparent cure of this case."[1]

" Reason—Virtue—Happiness, simply means: we must imitate Socrates and confront the dark passions permanently with the light of day—the light of reason. We must at all costs be clever, precise, clear: all yielding to the instincts, to the unconscious, leads downwards. . . ."[2]

Thus Nietzsche saw in Socrates " the type of *theoretical human being* " who, in unshakable optimism, believes " that thought, following the clues of causality, reaches even into the deepest abyss of Being, and that thought is able not only to recognize Being but also even to *correct* it." Socrates, as is well known, left no literary work, but was content to influence his pupils and disciples through " mere speech." In this technique, in its aim at self-knowledge, in its intuition that insight leads to virtue, and not least in its whole thera-peutic effect, one ought indeed to designate him as the primal father of the analytic technique, which found in Plato its worthy theorist. This comparison contains deep justifica-tion, when we remember that Socrates himself likened his dialectic therapy of drawing forth thoughts to the *practice of midwifery*, as he practises it in imitation of his mother,

[1] *Ibid.*, p. 14.   [2] *Ibid.*, p. 15.

who was a midwife. This anecdote, like the tradition of his evil wife Xanthippe, shows that in his case, and obviously from purely individual motives, that violent reaction to the primal trauma had set in, which apparently had made him the *type dégénéré* described by Nietzsche. The biological results of this, his ugliness, deformity, aural delusions, the unrestrained character of his instinctive life, as Nietzsche described it, become comprehensible in a flash. And the same may be said of his psychical reactions, in which he is obviously compelled, through his identification with the mother, to attain the detachment from the overstrong fixation on her, and to give himself up to the love of boys, in which he could constantly renew the lost mother-child relation. Finally, he succeeded in overcoming the birth trauma in yet a third way, namely, in overcoming the fear of death. As Nietzsche rightly recognized, Socrates voluntarily willed his death, since only banishment was customary for transgressions of his kind. He had willed it, and he *could will* it; " He appears to us as the first who could live not only under the guidance of that instinct of science, but—what is more important—could also die. And on that account the image of the *dying* Socrates, of the human being freed, through knowledge and reason, from the fear of death, is the armorial bearings which, over the entrance-door to science, reminds every one of its purpose, namely, to make existence seem comprehensible and justified."

Thus Socrates—although he undoubtedly made use of various partially neurotic compensatory gratifications, and although he had to pay the price by drinking hemlock—was the first who succeeded in intellectually overcoming the birth trauma, and thereby establishes his claim to be the forerunner of Psychoanalysis.

PSYCHOANALYTICAL KNOWLEDGE

WE have recognized from the analytic situation and the patient's unconscious representation of it the fundamental importance of the birth trauma, its repression and its return in neurotic reproduction, symbolic adaptation, heroic compensation, ethical reaction formation, æsthetic idealization, and philosophic speculation. We believe we have shown, in a bird's-eye view of the essential achievements and developments of civilization, that not only all socially valuable, even over-valued, creations of man but even the fact of becoming man, arise from a specific reaction to the birth trauma, and, finally, that recognition of this through the psychoanalytic method is due to the most complete removal as yet achieved of the primal repression, through the overcoming of the primal resistance, anxiety.

The development of psychoanalytic knowledge itself gives an instructive picture of the power of this primal resistance, and of Freud's stupendous accomplishment in overcoming it. As Freud continually emphasizes, the real discoverer of Psychoanalysis was not himself but the late Dr. Josef Breuer of Vienna, who in 1881 treated the case of hysteria mentioned above, and was thus brought by the patient to the idea of the *talking cure*, symbolically spoken of as *chimney sweeping*. When Freud incidentally among friends spoke of Breuer's part in Psychoanalysis, he betrayed very deep understanding, which likewise appears in the most personal of his works, *The History of the Psychoanalytic Movement* (1914), where he states that Breuer finally fled from the con-

sequences of this discovery, as from an *untoward event*,
because he did not want to recognize the sexual factor, the
courageous recognition of which helped Freud himself much
later to the understanding of his teacher's reaction.   And
the later secessions in the movement which took place among
the adherents of Psychoanalysis, and which had led to new
theories based not on observation but on opposition, Freud
himself characterized in the same publication as " regressive
movements struggling away from Psychoanalysis."   As he
himself sufficiently experienced, the last thing for which
human beings seem to be created is to bear psychoanalytic
truths, and he often said, when one or another of his disciples
refused to follow him any further, that it was not for everyone
to be continuously investigating the dark ravines of the
Unconscious with only an occasional glance at the light of
day.   One does not know which to admire most, Freud's
courage in discovery, or the fighting tenacity with which
he defended his findings against the resistances of the whole
world.   He defended them still more strenuously against
single fellow-workers who were close to him, and who,
horrified like Breuer at these discoveries, took to flight,
in the various directions in which they could see any hope
of escape from these opinions, disturbing to the sleep of the
world.   Whatever of value they found as a refuge on their
ways of retreat, Freud has distinguished with remarkable
objectivity from the distortions and denials of the truth only
imperfectly divined; but at the same time he has eliminated
them from his own field of work as not really " psychoanalytic."

   In the exaggerations and misunderstandings of the disciples
who have remained faithful to Freud, and who, after their
fashion, interpreted the master's teachings all too literally,

the history of the psychoanalytic movement shows the same oscillating picture as every intellectual movement which discloses the truth on one decisive point.   This decisive point was actually Breuer's discovery, from which Freud was undoubtedly the first to draw the practical and theoretical conclusions with equal consistency.   If, therefore; we are now trying to establish a direct connection with Breuer's discovery, it is in order to show both how logical Freud himself was in all his views, and also how the concept brought forward here logically completes Breuer's discovery, and Freud's conception and elaboration of it.

Breuer's starting-point was " the fundamental fact that the symptoms of hysterical patients depend on impressive but forgotten scenes of their life (traumata), the therapy based on it causing them to remember and to reproduce these experiences under hypnosis (catharsis), and the consequent fragment of theory, that these symptoms correspond to an abnormal use of undischarged quantities of excitation (conversion)."   If into this Freudian definition[1] of the nucleus of Breuer's primal discovery we insert the birth trauma, which is repeated and solved in the cure, the psychophysiological starting-point of analysis from the problem of " conversion " (Freud) seems to be connected with the likewise psychophysical factor of the birth trauma.   What lies in between is the psychology of the Unconscious created by Freud alone, namely, the first psychology which at all deserves this independent name, since the academic psychology originating from philosophical speculation gradually encroached more and more on to medical ground (philosophy of the senses, neurology, anatomy of the brain).

[1] " The History of the Psychoanalytic Movement," *Coll. Papers,* vol. i., p. 289.

Now we understand better how the first difference arose between Breuer's " physiological " concept, the " hypnoid theory," and Freud's purely psychological concept, " the doctrine of defence," which then led to the discovery of repression and, further, to the investigation of the repressed (preconscious—unconscious), and finally to the repressing forces of the Ego (and its derivatives, conscience, guilt-feeling, ideal-formation, etc.).

It is not only interesting from an historical scientific point of view but also from the human point of view, that the separation of Freud from Breuer concerned the psycho-physical borders of " conversion." The name, indeed, originates from Freud, but the fact yielded itself, as Freud stated, " simultaneously and in common " to the two investigators. It is as though this ground of division, the severance of the pupil from his master, had been tabooed ever since, for not only has the problem of conversion remained unsolved till today, but scarcely a pupil has ventured to approach it.[1] If, by consistently following the Freudian method, we are driven back on to this analytic primal problem, we are fully conscious of the responsibility which the attempt to solve it bears, but we believe our point of view to be sufficiently justified by the universal import-ance which we have shown it to possess.

In the course of our arguments we have evaded the ques-tion as to how it comes about that the striving for the recovery of the pleasurable primal situation in the womb, recognized as the primal tendency of the libido and regarded by us as an expression of the greatest possibility of pleasure,

---

[1] With the exception of Ferenczi (*Hysterie und Pathoneurosen*, 1919), who conceives conversion to have a meaning similar to ours, namely, " regression to the proto-psyche " (*l.c.*, p. 24).

is bound up in so inseparable a way with the primal anxiety, as shown by the anxiety dream, neurotic symptoms, and also by all derivative and related formations. In order to understand this we must bear in mind that the pleasurable primal state is interrupted through the act of birth—presumably also shortly before, through displacement and pressure (movements of the child)—in unwished-for ways, and that the rest of life consists in replacing this lost paradise in the above described highly complicated roundabout ways of the libido, the primal state being actually no longer attainable.

It would seem that the primal anxiety-affect at birth, which remains operative through life, right up to the final separation from the outer world (gradually become a second mother) at death, is from the very beginning not merely an expression of the new-born child's physiological injuries (dyspnœa—constriction—anxiety), but in consequence of the change from a highly pleasurable situation to an extremely painful one, immediately acquires a " psychical " quality of feeling.   This *experienced* anxiety is thus the first content of perception, the first psychical act, so to say, to set up barriers; and in these we must recognize the primal repression against the already powerful tendency to re-establish the pleasurable situation just left. Conversion, the normal forms of which Freud recognized in the so-called physical expression of emotion, thus proves to be identical with the emergence of the psychical out of physical innervations, namely, with the conscious impression of the perceived primal anxiety. If this were purely physiological, it probably could sooner or later be completely removed; but it is psychically anchored in this way in order to prevent the backward striving tendency of the libido, which then, in all later circumstances where anxiety develops, breaks itself against this barrier wall of the primal repression. That is, the perceived and psychically fixed impression of the primal anxiety blots out the memory of the former pleasurable state, and with this, prevents regression which would make us unfit for life, as is shown in the "brave" suicide, who contrives to pass this anxiety barrier retrogressively. It seems as though man were completely unable to bear this painful separation from the primal object, and as if, moreover, he would not accomplish the compensatory adjustment to reality without being held back from a far-reaching regression by a threatening repetition of the primal anxiety. As soon as one approaches this barrier—whether it be in sleep (dream) or in waking life (unconscious phantasies)—anxiety appears, and this explains the unconscious pleasurable character as well as the conscious painful character of all neurotic symptoms. The only real possibility of an approximate reinstatement of the primal pleasure is given in sexual union, in the partial and purely physical return into the womb. But this partial gratification, to which is joined the highest sensation of pleasure, does not satisfy every individual. More correctly expressed, some individuals, owing to a stronger influence of the birth trauma derived from the germ plasm and to a consequently stronger primal repression (reaction), can establish this partial physical relationship to the object only in a more or less unsatisfying way. Their Unconscious strives to reproduce the complete return, sometimes through the establishment of complete physical identity of mother and child with the sexual partner (masturbation, homosexuality),[1] sometimes by

[1] Martial said of the homosexual: *pars est una patris cetera matris habent.*

means of the defence mechanism of identification in neurotic symptoms, instead of attaining this through the consummation of the sexual act, and through the creation of a new living being with whom they can identify themselves. Here lies, moreover, the fundamental difference in the whole psychical development of man and woman. The woman is in the position, through a complete reproduction of the primal situation, namely, through actual repetition of pregnancy and parturition, to procure for herself the most far-reaching approach to the primal gratification, whilst the man, here depending on unconscious identification, has to create for himself a substitute for this reproduction, by identifying himself with the " mother " and the creation resulting from it of cultural and artistic productions. This explains the lesser part played by woman in cultural development, from which, then, her social under - valuation follows as a secondary effect, whilst virtually the whole creation of civilization has only resulted from man's libidinal over-estimation of the maternal primal object and from its elimination through the primal repression.[1] Thus one could say that the normal social adjustment corresponds to an extensive transference of the primal libido to that which is paternal and creative, whilst everything pathological (but also supernormal) rests on an all too strong mother fixation or the defence reaction against it. In between lies complete sexual gratification, which also includes the wish for children, and allows an almost complete conversion of the primal anxiety back into primal libido; hence the numerous dis-

[1] Here lies the deepest motivation for the idea brought forward as the *primum movens* by Alfred Adler, of the " inferiority " of woman, which, moreover, is a direct consequence of the repression of the birth trauma, quite independently of sex.

turbances possible within the complicated sexual mechanism likewise release anxiety, which, in the case of direct disturbances of the sexual function (Freud's "actual neuroses"), immediately becomes free, whereas in the case of the psychically anchored psychoneuroses, on the other hand, it seems bound by the protective structure of symptoms, and in every kind of attack the anxiety is discharged by reproduction.

Thus, with the birth trauma and the fœtal condition preceding it, we have at last made tangible the much-disputed border of the psychophysical, and from this we understand not only anxiety, that primal symptom of mankind, but also conversion, as well as the entire life of the affects and impulses which take root in the psychophysical. Impulse is actually nothing but the immediate reaction to the psychically anchored primal anxiety; it is, so to say, instinct modified by it. For the Ego, in its retreat from the confines of anxiety, is constantly *urged* forwards to seek for Paradise in the world formed in the image of the mother, instead of seeking it in the past, and, in so far as this fails, to look for it in the sublime wish compensations of religion, art, and philosophy. In reality this enormous task of adaptation, in so far as it is a matter of the creation of genuine values, is successfully accomplished by only one type of human being, which the history of mind has handed down to us as the hero, but which we would like to designate as "artist" in the broadest sense of the word,[1] in so far as it is a question of a creation of ideal values, of phantastic superstructure, created from the remains of primal libido unsatisfied in real creation. Thus the normal man is born

[1] Rank, *Der Künstler, Ansätze zu einer Sexualpsychologie*, 1907, 2nd edition, 1918.

into a world which already represents the primal symbol, and finding ready-made forms of gratification in conformity with the general average of repression, he has only to perceive *again* and make use of these out of his own primal experience (symbolism).

This is the place to draw one of the most important theoretical conclusions from our concept, which in any case proves to be a quite direct continuation of the investigation made by Freud. From the very beginning, the specific analytic point of view put in the background for the time being all hereditary and phylogenetic influences. For one thing, these were to a great extent difficult to grasp, and Psychoanalysis corrected the immoderate overvaluation to which they were submitted by making accessible to investigation a large and highly important part of individual development, namely, early childhood, which was thus shown to be a determining factor of very great importance. But since the development of the analytic technique has enabled us in the course of our experience to trace this infantile stage of development ever further back, till finally we reach the pre-natal stage, it follows—especially from a more thorough-going study of dream symbolism—that we may dispense with the phylogenetic point of view of an inherited *psychical* endowment or can limit it, in Haeckel's sense, to the bio-genetic fundamental law. Hence all problems of symbolism are explained in a simpler and more satisfying manner than by Jung's untimely introduction of the phylogenetic point of view into analysis; for, being purely a psychiatrist and using mythological material as a comparison, he lacked the real experience of the analysis of neuroses which would have allowed him to go beyond mere description and the speculation connected with it. Freud likewise recognized

the unproductiveness of Jung's attempt to explain the
phenomena of individual psychology by means of uninter-
preted ethnological material, and he pursued the only
correct way, which we now pursue still further and thus
place the phylogenetic point of view considerably further in
the background.

After having been able to trace the *primal phantasies* of
castration and the Œdipus situation back to the birth
trauma (separation), or to its pleasurable previous stage
(reunion with the mother), it was not difficult, referring
directly to Freud's observations, to trace to its real substratum the pre-natal situation, the spying on the parental
intercourse as a typical situation, embracing both separation
and reunion with the mother.   Already in the second edition
of *The Interpretation of Dreams* Freud mentions typical
dreams, " at the basis of which lie phantasies of the intrauterine life, namely, dwelling in the mother's womb and
parturition " (p. 198).   He gives as one of the examples
the dream of a young man, " who in phantasy already uses
the intrauterine occasion for spying on the intercourse
between the parents."   This, as well as the next communi-
cated birth dream of a patient who must *separate* herself
from the analyst, is, as Freud first recognized, a dream of
the analytic cure, from the regular occurrence of which our
investigation took its starting-point.   With reference to
the healing situation, indeed, they correspond to phantasies,
which, however, only correspond to the reflex of an actual
reproduction of the birth act with real " remembered "
material.   Many years later, after the so-called " womb
phantasy," long scoffed at by all critics, had maintained its
place in Psychoanalysis, Freud again followed up this
problem in his classical presentation of the history of an

infantile neurosis,[1] and obstinately defended the certainly incomprehensible reality of the "primal scene," not only against the attempts of former disciples to re-interpret it, but even against his own scientific doubt. Starting from the analytical rebirth phantasies of the patient, whose complaints "that the world seemed to him disguised by a veil" could be traced back to his birth in a caul, Freud came to the conclusion that the patient wished himself back in the womb (*l.c.*, p. 580), in order there, in identification with the mother, to be fertilized by the father, and to bear him a child. The first part of the wish, as we can show by indisputable evidence, is really to be taken biologically; the second part shows the degree of disguise and elaboration which this original wish tendency has suffered through the specific experience of the boy in childhood. In a footnote (*l.c.*, p. 695) Freud himself designates this question of the power of remembering back as "the most ticklish of the whole analytic doctrine," and comes to the conclusion that "a kind of knowledge difficult to define, perhaps a sort of preparation for understanding, operates in the child in the reactivation of the primal scene. What this consists in we have no idea; we have at our disposal only the one excellent analogy of the far-reaching *instinctive* knowledge of animals" (*l.c.*, p. 604). The fact that in the completely uninfluenced dreams at the beginning of analysis, conforming, moreover, to the general type of dream of the person in question, in addition to the spying out situation re-phantasied from hearsay or facts, there are purely biological elements (as position of the limbs, particular birth pains, etc.) which cannot have been known by the mother, yet can be proved in connection with the physical symptoms of the

[1] *Coll. Papers*, vol. iii., Case Histories, v.

neurosis, and place us in the position of comprehending the real foundation of the " spying out " phantasy.[1] For this we need only follow again the already described manner of " symbolic " adjustment to reality from the parental bed-room, to which the scene is mostly transferred, to its real prototype, the womb situation.   In this way the real essence of the " primal phantasy," namely, the fact that it is a matter of indifference whether the scene was experienced or not, becomes intelligible without further ado, for even the observed coitus could not have the traumatic effect if the patient were not reminded of the primal trauma, the first disturbance of the blessed peace by the father.   So the later childish Œdipus complex proves to be an immediate derivative, that is, the psychosexual elaboration of the intrauterine Œdipus situation—which thus proves to be the " nuclear complex of the neuroses," since this paternal disturbance, although not the first " trauma," yet deserves to be called its immediate forerunner.[2]

From these points of view the real substratum of the " primal phantasies " becomes tangible, the primal reality which lies at the bottom of them is shown up, and so the " psychical reality " which we, like Freud, must ascribe to the Unconscious, is to be grasped and understood as a bio-logical reality.   We can provisionally renounce the assump-

---

[1] The phantastic element therein, the throwing back of the heterosexual stage, has found its precipitate in obscene jokes as well as in numerous mythical traditions, where the hero has inter-course while still in the womb (Osiris).

[2] Hence it cannot be altogether a matter of indifference up to what time sexual intercourse is continued during pregnancy. *Cf.* the late Dr. Hug-Hellmuth's argument (*A Study of the Mental Life of the Child*), where it is hinted that small children's joy in rhythm is in actual relation to the fœtal experiences of movement in the womb.

tion of an inherited psychical content, for that which is primarily psychical, the real *Unconscious*, proves to be the *embryonal* state *existing unchanged in the adult Ego*.[1] By this embryonal I mean that which Psychoanalysis has recently described in a meta-psychological term as the idea of the sexually neuter " It." Everything which goes beyond this embryonal, especially everything sexual in the narrow sense, belongs to the preconscious, as also indeed the sexual symbolism used in wit, folklore, and myth shows; the real Unconscious consists only in the libidinal relation of the embryo to the womb.

From this definition of the Unconscious all those characteristics can easily be explained, which, according to Freud's last contribution to the subject,[2] form the real unconscious kernel of our Ego; first of all the wish tendency, unchangeable in its intensity and unable to be satisfied, which Freud has comprehended as the striving of the libido to re-establish a lost primal condition; then the " narcissistic " primal character of this situation, the absolute lack of sex differentiation, whereby originally every object opposed to the Ego contains the mother character; further, the timelessness and the lack of every negation, which is " first introduced by the process of repression,"[3] and therefore originates in the psychical experience of the birth trauma; finally, the funda-

---

[1] A proof of this is the fact, known analytically but not yet understood, that the same symbols are used in dreams to represent the Unconscious and the womb (room, building, cupboard, ravines, hollows); these symbols Silberer was able to grasp only as psychical self manifestations of the Unconscious. See his last work referring to this in the report of the Vienna group (*Int. Zschr. f. Ps.A.* viii., 1922, p. 536).

[2] Freud, *The Ego and the Id*.

[3] See " The History of an Infantile Neurosis," *Coll. Papers*, vol. iii., p. 559, note 2.

mental psychical mechanism of the Unconscious, (a) the striving for *projection*, decisive for the development of cultural adjustment which has to replace the lost condition in the outer world; and (b) the enigmatic inclination to *identification*, which again aims at the setting up of the old identity with the mother.

Also the complete lack of negation *per se*—*i.e.*, the idea of death—belongs essentially to the character of the Unconscious, and is of the highest importance for the understanding of the whole life process, as Freud soon discovered in his studies of infantile life.   The child and its psychical representative, the Unconscious, knows only of the situation before birth, given to it in experience, the pleasurable remembrance of which continues in the indestructible belief in immortality, in the idea of an everlasting life after death. But what biologically seems to us the impulse to death, strives again to establish nothing else than the already experienced condition before birth, and the " compulsion to repetition "[1] arises from the unquenchable character of this longing, which exhausts itself again and again in every possibility of form.   This process is what biologically speaking we call " life."   If in the course of life the " normal " individual, detached by the birth trauma, amidst the difficulties of the child's development and by the avoidance of neurotic relapses, succeeds in adjusting himself to the outer world as " the best of all worlds," namely, as a mother substitute, it is nevertheless clear that the Unconscious has, in the meantime, pursued with tenacious perseverance the

---

[1] See Freud's *Beyond the Pleasure Principle*.   With the conception here represented, Roheim's summary remarks at the end of his series of articles almost entirely coincide, " Das Selbst " (*Imago*, vii., 1921, p. 503 ff.).

regressive way which was prescribed for it, and which still leads it back to its original goal against the will of the Ego. But this process, which we call " ageing," has, in order to attain the unconscious aim, to apply itself to the systematic destruction of the whole body, which, through all kinds of illnesses, it finally leads to death.[1] At the moment of dying, the body once more severs itself from the mother substitute, " Dame World," whose front is comely and beautifully formed, but whose back is thought to be ugly and horrible.[2] This separation is still easy for the Unconscious,[3] as it is only a matter of giving up one substitute for the attainment of real blessedness. Here is not only the root of the popular idea of death as deliverer, but also the essential factor in all religious ideas of deliverance. On the other hand, the fearful idea of death as a scythe-bearer, who severs one sharply from life, is to be traced back to the primal anxiety which man reproduces for the last time in the last trauma, in the last breath at death, and so gains from the greatest anxiety, namely, that of death, the pleasure

[1] *Cf.* the Buddhistic Evils, Age, Disease, Death. Socrates said, when he took the cup of poison: " *Life—that is to be long ill ;* I owe a cock as sacrifice to the saviour Asklepios." (Naturally, the mythical saviour Asklepios is a deity of rebirth, who was punished by Zeus in being killed by lightning because he had *awakened a dead person.*)

[2] See " Frau Welt " by H. Niggemann (*Mitra*, i., 1914, No. 10, p. 279).

[3] Hufeland, the great doctor and observer of men, speaks of the apparent painfulness of dying. In an essay which accidentally came to my notice during the writing of this work Heinz Welten (*Über Land und Meer*, April, 1923) shows in the traditional last words of our great men " how easily one dies." Goethe's now famous utterance, " More light," shows clearly the unconscious birth phantasy, the wish to look at the light of the world. Goethe's abnormally difficult birth trauma, of which he himself speaks, explains that which was so puzzling in his life and works.

of denying death by again undergoing the birth anxiety.
How seriously the Unconscious conceives dying as a return
to the womb may be concluded from the death-rites of all
nations and times, which punish the disturbance of the
eternal sleep (through the father) as the greatest iniquity
and the most malicious crime.

As the soul, according to the profound dogma of the
Church Fathers, passes into the embryo only at an advanced
stage of pregnancy when the child is able to perceive the
first impressions, so it leaves the body in death, to become
participator in immortal life.   In this separation of the soul
from the body the unquenchable wish attempts to recover
immortality.   Here once more we stumble on the original,
apparently phantastic, but in reality perfectly genuine
content of the idea of the soul, which, according to the skilful
arguments of Rohde's *Psyche*, developed from the idea of
death.   The soul is originally imagined to be endowed with
a body, a second self of the deceased (the Egyptian Ka and
parallel forms),[1] which has to replace him after death in the
meaning of a quite real survival.   How the religious idea of
a soul and the philosophical soul concept have developed
from the primitive belief in souls I have attempted incidentally to portray in another connection.[2]   Psychoanalytic
investigation, which has unmasked all these creations as
unconscious wish phantasies, now turns back again to seize
the real soul content, as it is realized in the ever-recurring
embryonal state.

In the face of all these sublime, constantly renewed

[1] F. S. Krauss, Sreća, *Glück und Schicksal im Volksglauben der
Südslaven*, Wien, 1886. The same, " Der Doppelgängerglaube im
alten Ägypten und bei den Südslaven " (*Imago*, vi., 1920, p. 387 ff.).
Rank, " Der Doppelgänger " (*Imago*, iii., 1914).

[2] " Die Don Juan-Gestalt " (*Imago*, vii., 1922, p. 166 ff.).

attempts to re-establish by means of the most varied forms of substitutional gratification the lost primal state, and to deny the primal trauma, one can for a moment understand the whole wavering course of history, with its apparently arbitrary and changing phases, as subject to the conditions of biological law. The same mechanism is here at work which was so magnificently elaborated from the primal repression.

Times of great external distress, which remind the Unconscious too strongly of the individual's first affliction in life, namely, the birth trauma, lead automatically to increased regressive attempts which must again be given up, not only because they never can achieve the real aim, but just because they have approached too near to it and have come up against the primal anxiety, which keeps watch in front of Paradise, like the Cherubim who hold the flashing sword before its gates. So the primal tendency to re-establish the first and most pleasurable experience is opposed not only by the primal repression, acting as a protection against the repetition of the most painful experience associated with it, but simultaneously also by the striving against the source of pleasure itself, of which one does not wish to be reminded because it must remain unattainable. In the erection of this *double barrier of repression,* which corresponds to the prevention of the memory of the primal pleasure through the birth anxiety, and to the forgetting of the painful birth trauma by remembering the previous pleasure experience, in other words, in this *primal ambivalence* of the psychical, is answered the riddle of human development, which could be solved in only one way, namely, through the discovery by Psychoanalysis of the process of repression itself.

THE THERAPEUTIC ASPECT

WHEN we bring to mind the power of the primal repression (once more in evidence at the close of the previous chapter) and the attempts to overcome it repeated by man indefatigably and ever fruitlessly throughout thousands of years, our first inclination might be to add to the pessimistic consequences to which this concept seems everywhere to lead, the thought of the hopelessness of all psycho-therapy. For what power on earth could prevail upon the Unconscious to renounce its inborn nature and to take another direction ? From what has been said no other conclusion seems possible than that there can be no such power. On the other hand, analytic experience shows that something must exist which makes it possible to an extensive degree to free highly neurotic human beings from the excessive dominance of their Unconscious and put them in a position to live as those do who are not neurotic. That, to be sure, is all that can be done. It is very much and at the same time very little, according to the point of view from which one considers the result. Now apparently only the analyst himself is inclined to consider it from the first point of view, whilst the patient frequently enough can judge it only from the second. This contradiction, indeed, seems at first to need no further explanation, but yet it deserves to be investigated with regard to its psychological motivation.

It is not a question of cases where the analyst may believe with subjective justification that he has done not only his best but everything, and where a real success actually fails to appear. I have rather cases in mind where the patient is actually freed from his suffering, is again made capable of work and enjoyment, and yet behaves like a discontented person. Yet in spite of this we must neither be discouraged in our task nor become irresolute. For who can say that all the other people who have not undergone an analysis, in whom perhaps it is not at all necessary, are more contented or more happy ? We remember a remark of Freud's in which he stated that the cured neurotic often shows afterwards only ordinary unhappiness, where he previously had " neurotic " unhappiness ! In the case of severe physical diseases the doctor can scarcely fulfil the patient's demands for perfect health, much less then in the case of the neurotic, who is ill just because of the excess of his claims and, indeed, of those libidinal claims which according to their very nature and according to psychoanalytic knowledge never can be gratified. This latter-day knowledge of the causes of neurosis tends, therefore, to make us give up every attempt to cure it, instead of giving into our hands, along with the knowledge of its causation, the means for its removal. And is not this the most complete nihilism in psycho-therapy—nay, more, a denial of that spirit of scientific enquiry which is the modern practical application of the Socratic saying, " Knowledge is power " ?

Now in the first place Psychoanalysis has in fact shaken this prejudice which is handed down from its ancient forerunner as the sum of wisdom. Psychoanalysis has compelled us step by step to lay aside our intellectual pride and to learn to attach less and less value to the power of our consciousness as against the biological and elementary force of the Unconscious. I believe we have to go further along the same way in the field of psychoanalytic therapy itself.

After having acquired sufficient knowledge, we are able to recognize—modifying Socrates' statement—that all we know is that our knowledge is not of much value therapeutically if we are not able to apply it effectively. Freud himself soon warned us against confusing our own knowledge and understanding with that of the patient,[1] in that he sharply distinguished between Psychoanalysis as a method of investigation and as therapy. So long as we had found out so little about the Unconscious, investigation was often unavoidably pushed into the foreground at a time when existing knowledge was not sufficient for the attainment of therapeutic effects. But the fruitful experiences of the last few years have convinced us that therapeutic possibilities do not conform, in any expected degree, to the increase of our knowledge, and that even simple therapeutic action can be arrested by too much knowledge and too much insight.[2] On the other hand, experience has long shown that the communication of our knowledge to the patients, and even their intellectual acceptance of it, in no way changes their symptoms. Analysis had to ascribe therapeutic value to the affective acceptance which was finally equivalent to abreacting the affects, and was possible only after the removal of unconscious resistances. In place of conscious memories, such as were allowed in the old days of hypnosis, there soon appeared repetition in positive and negative transference, to which was attached real affective reproduction.[3] It was

[1] " Further Recommendations in the Technique of Psychoanalysis," Coll. Papers, vol. ii., p. 362.
[2] Such experiences seem to have been the reason for Professor Freud making at the last Psychoanalytic Congress (September, 1922,) " The Relation of Psychoanalytic Theory to Technique," the subject for a prize essay.
[3] " Further Recommendations in the Technique of Psychoanalysis. Recollection, Repetition, and Working Through," Coll.

further apparent that one has by no means to avoid this, but often rather to provoke it, as when the patient uses his memory as a guard against repetition, *i.e.* in its biological function. As is well known, Ferenczi was the first vigorously to indicate the necessity for an " active " therapy;[1] he then sought to justify this view in a thorough presentation, and to give it a basis against misunderstandings.[2] He rightly emphasized the fact that the activity criticized as an innovation has been at all times silently practised in Psychoanalysis, and I know of no further argument to add than that all therapy, by nature, is " active," that is it purposes an effect through volitional influence and a change resulting from it. The passivity rightly commended in Psychoanalysis is a virtue in the investigator, and places him, moreover, in a position to find something new which he does not yet know. Just as little as the specialist at a patient's bedside need refer to the history of medicine or even to a text-book in order to form a correct diagnosis, need the practical analyst take his patient, step by step, through the whole development of psychoanalytic investigation and unroll historically his patient's psychical life. He has rather to absorb in the right way the sum of all knowledge achieved so far, and then to apply it to the demands of the case in a practical way. That in this he must proceed " actively " is obvious if he aims at attaining any therapeutic effect worthy of the name. His intervention is no less active than that of the surgeon,

---

Papers, vol. ii. *Cf.* Ferenczi and Rank, *The Development of Psychoanalysis*.

[1] " Technische Schwierigkeiten einer Hysterieanalyse," *Int. Zschr. f. Ps.A.*, v., 1919.

[2] " Weiterer Ausbau der 'aktiven Technik' in der Ps.a," *ibid.*, vii., 1921.

and has for its aim the correct severance of the primal libido from its fixation, by the removal or the lessening of the primal repression, and with it the freeing of the patient from his neurotic fixation; and this ultimately means going back to a repetition of the birth trauma, with the help of an experienced midwife. I have purposely avoided writing " doctor," because I want to emphasize the purely human and practical factor of the process.

If we linger for a moment longer and consider this newly fixed therapeutic aim, we shall see with satisfaction the first gleam of hope in the darkness of therapeutic pessimism into which we seem to have landed. We shall recognize then that we have really done nothing more than that which the patient has attempted his whole life long only with insufficient success, namely, to overcome the birth trauma in the sense of adjustment. According to our conception the new-born individual would immediately fall back into the abandoned state, that is, practically expressed, would die, unless Nature undertook the first " therapeutic " intervention and prevented the striving back by the anchoring of anxiety. From this moment every further activity of the individual in life acquires a " therapeutic " character, in that, in opposition to the backward striving tendencies, it preserves the " abandoned " patients for a while longer in life, without however succeeding in this for ever. We should like here to point out the high " cathartic " value possessed by just those manifestations possessing least obvious utility, namely, the activities expressing unconscious tendencies, from childish games[1] to grown-up people's play which in tragedy reaches its highest cathartic development. Indeed, as Freud

[1] See Karl Groos, " Das Spiel als Katharsis," *Zschr. f. pädag. Psychologie*, xii., 1912.

was able to show in the caricature in the psychoses, we have to consider their course rather as an attempt at healing which, like that of Analysis, shows up regressive tendencies. Analysis, moreover, must follow up these tendencies if it wishes to gain the possibility of influencing them. But it is in the position to grant the patient just enough pleasure not to endanger the final weaning from the libido-misuse. Psychoanalysis thus replaces for the patient, in the way already described, the lost primal object, the mother, by a surrogate, whom he learns to renounce the more easily by being continually made conscious of the surrogate as such. The great value which this surrogate has for him, nevertheless, and which is expressed in the phenomenon of the trans-ference, lies in its reality, namely, in the fact that the analyst allows the patient not only to fix his libido on him for a while, but directly provokes this through the conditions and arrangements of the cure. So the neurotic introversion is paralyzed by the analytic situation, and the remedy which Psychoanalysis uses is the human being who, in a way similar to the magical practices of the medicine-man, works by appealing directly to the patient's Unconscious.[1] If one likes to call this suggestion, there is nothing to object to it beyond the fact that one has replaced a process at present psychologically intelligible by an empty technical term.[2]

Not only analytic therapy, but every therapy, every medica-ment finally operates in the same sense " suggestively," that is in so far as it impresses the patient's Unconscious. This is already expressed in the choice of, or in the personal relation

[1] See in addition the folklore material, rich in content, appearing to me, however, to be expounded in too complicated a way by Roheim, " Nach dem Tode des Urvaters " (*Imago*, ix., 1, 1923).

[2] See Freud, " The Dynamics of Transference," *Coll. Papers*, vol. ii., p. 319.

to, the doctor, which invariably rests on transference[1] and thus indirectly lends the necessary weight of the Unconscious to his therapeutic measures. But from numerous experiences in analyses, we are in a position to elucidate this Unconscious effect of the transference in its mechanism. We know that in the child's life the " doctor " plays a quite definite part, which clearly comes to light in the familiar game of doctor; he represents the child's unconscious ideal in so far as he certainly seems to know whence children come and also what goes on in the inside of the body. Whether he listens and knocks, tests the excretions or operates with the knife, he always vaguely arouses the primal trauma. The psychoanalytic situation, in which this transference must be made conscious, shows us with complete clearness to what degree the Unconscious of the most grown-up human beings has remained fixed the whole life long on the " doctor game," which is directly related to birth. Indeed, every patient behaves in a manifest way like a frightened child in a dark room, that is he calms down, as is well known, immediately the doctor appears and speaks to him consolingly. Although at present the majority of doctors do not wish to acknowledge this—and perhaps many cannot, as they themselves still " play doctor " in the Unconscious too much—because they fear an injury to their scientific reputation, yet they might learn from the few analytically influenced medical specialists and doctors, to whom the serious recognition and practical use of this fact has brought much unexpected success. But analysis, which has led not merely to the recognition of this fact but also to the enlightenment of the patient about it, seems to prove that this, far from being

[1] See Ferenczi, " Introjection and Transference," *Contributions to Psychoanalysis*, p. 30.

harmful, is the only possibility of giving a lasting effect to therapeutic success. For this *severance from the analyst*, which is the *essential part* of the analytic work, is accomplished by reproduction of the birth trauma, so that the patient loses his doctor and his suffering at the same time, or, better expressed, must give up his doctor in order to lose his suffering.

The understanding of this parallel process leads to the real question concerning the healing process, its mechanism, and the technique which one has to use therein. Now these problems can be studied only from the material itself and its detailed analysis, which I intend to publish very shortly.[1] But, quite briefly, I would like to circumscribe the part of the Unconscious on the one hand and of conscious knowledge, so often misunderstood, on the other.

We must here especially guard ourselves from falling into " Socratism," rightly criticized by Nietzsche, and constituting a danger which Socrates himself finally escaped only with effort. We are all always far too " theoretical," and are inclined to think that knowledge alone makes us virtuous. That is not the case, as Psychoanalysis has proved. Knowledge is something entirely different from the healing factor. The depths of the Unconscious can, according to the latter's very nature, be changed just as little as the other organs necessary for life. The only result we can attain in Psychoanalysis is a *changed attitude of the Ego to the Unconscious*. But this means very much—indeed, as the history of man's development shows, practically everything. For man's psychical health and power of

---

[1] See for the present, " Zum Verständnis der Libidoentwicklung im Heilungsvorgang," *Zschr.*, ix., 4, 1923.

achievement depend on the relation of his Ego to the Unconscious.[1] In normally efficient men the various inhibiting Ego elements, which correspond to the Socratic " dæmon," are in a position to keep the Unconscious in check through critical condemnation and moderate emotional rejection (conscience and guilt feeling). In neuroses of the hysterical type, a stronger means, namely the anxiety of the primal trauma, must again and again be mobilized, in order to prevent the Unconscious from drawing back into regression the Ego which has arisen from it. In neuroses of the obsessional type the same effect is attained through hypertrophy of the Ego elements; whilst in psychoses we have before us the terrible result which occurs when the Unconscious proves to be too powerful and the Ego too weak. The sphere in which Psychoanalysis can be therapeutically effective includes all those cases in which it is a question of so regulating the relation of the Ego to the Unconscious, that through an adequate distribution of libido and anxiety, there results a harmonious relationship which we denote as normal adjustment. This sphere not only embraces all neurotic disturbances and the initial states of the psychoses,[2] but also everything which one could denote as psychical " secondary affects "—that is, sexual conflicts—and, to a certain extent, character abnormalities. Thus are included

[1] See Freud's last work, *The Ego and the Id*, 1923.

[2] I have the impression that at this point therapeutic possibilities could open up psychoses, as the points of view here explained seem to offer the first indication for an essentially simplified therapeutic operation capable of more immediate effect. The neuroses of simple men and the primitive content of psychoses compel one to look also for a simpler way of influencing them. I refer here to the well-known clinical fact, that mentally diseased women often show an improvement after the birth of a child; but also the reverse cases, the puerperal psychoses allow us to recognize the connections outlined above.

not only the crude disturbances of the relation between the Ego and the Unconscious, but also a number of finer functional disturbances within this relationship.

Taking into consideration the importance of the birth trauma, a new theory of character and types may be formed which has the advantage over existing attempts of this kind of giving a far-reaching understanding of the *individual* determinants and, consequently, the possibility of influencing them.[1] To these introverted and extroverted types (the names originated by Jung) correspond similar types of character, which may likewise be derived from the primal trauma or from the reaction to it. The introverted type of character seems to cling to the weak, delicate, fragile children, who are often born early and for the most part have an easy birth, whilst the nine-month and hence mostly stronger children frequently show the opposite type of character. This is explained by the fact that in the former, in consequence of the relatively slight birth trauma, the primal anxiety is not so powerful and the backward striving tendency has less resistance opposed to it; if these human beings become neurotic they generally show an introverted depressive character. The second type drive the intensely experienced primal anxiety forcefully outside, and they tend in their neuroses to reproduce less the primal situation than the birth trauma itself, against which, in their striving backwards, they violently collide.

Whilst we believe we have reached the first trauma-producing neuroses, we must be careful not to fall into an error which Psychoanalysis, through Freud's clear observations and thought, has repeatedly avoided. Just as the

---

[1] See for example Kretschmer, *Körperbau und Charakter*, 1921, or Jung, *Psychological Types*, 1921.

earliest "traumata," which one was inclined to make responsible for neurotic symptoms, prove to be a universal human normal experience, and as finally the analytically discovered nucleus of neuroses, the Œdipus complex, has been recognized as the typical normal attitude of the child and civilized man, so also is the last analytically comprehensible trauma, the trauma of birth, the most universal human experience. From this the process of development of the individual and of mankind is to be derived and explained in the way already described. It is obviously no mere coincidence that, again and again, as soon as we think we have found the key to the understanding of the neuroses, this changes itself in our hands into an instrument which seems still better fitted to unlock the hitherto unknown psychology of the normal. Thus Freud's main work may be explained as really signifying the first understanding of normal psychological phenomena (dream, wit, everyday life, sexual theory), the creation of the first general psychology, which certainly was gained from pathological material, and, indeed, by means of psychoanalytic method and technique generally. And so we would like to regard our arguments concerning the importance of the trauma of birth for Psychoanalysis only as a contribution to the Freudian structure of normal psychology, at best as one of its pillars. At the same time, we feel confident of having considerably furthered the doctrine of neuroses—including their therapy.

But we want to make quite clear to ourselves how far this has succeeded, because on it depends the further course which investigation must take. We believe that we have succeeded in recognizing all forms and symptoms of neurosis as expressions of a regression from the stage of sexual adjustment to the pre-natal primal state, or to the birth situation, which must be thereby overcome. For medical understanding and for therapeutic intervention this insight must by no means be underestimated, although in reference to the theory of neurosis it may have remained unsatisfying, in the meaning indicated above, since it traces what is specific in the case, or in the symptom formation, to something so universal as the birth trauma. On the other hand, within the birth trauma, there is room and to spare for hereditary influences of the germ plasm as also for incidental individual peculiarities of parturition. Nevertheless, our concept attempts to replace the theory of different places of fixation, which are supposed to determine the choice of neurosis, by *one* traumatic injury (producing various forms of reactions) in a single place of fixation namely, the mother (parturition). There is then, according to our view, only one fixation place, namely, the maternal body, and all symptoms ultimately relate to this primal fixation, which is given to us in the psychobiological fact of our Unconscious. In this sense we believe we have discovered in the trauma of birth the primal trauma. There is, therefore, no need to ascertain the "pathogenic traumata" in single cases by the lengthy way of analytic investigation, but only to recognize the specific birth trauma in reproduction, and demonstrate it to the patient's adult Ego as an infantile fixation. In reproduction the consoling mechanism effective in the birth trauma (best known from the examination dream: " also at that time it ended well !'") supplies a healing factor which should not be underestimated and which justifies optimism in the therapeutic sphere.

Although our new insight into the essence and character of the Unconscious (the It) has an eminently *practical* advantage, we must admit, with regard to the *doctrine* of neurosis, that from this point the *theory* of neurosis has yet to develop. But first of all we have recognized the neuroses in all their manifold forms as reproductions of, and reactions to, the birth trauma, and this gives us the foundation for normal cultural adaptation as well as for all man's higher achievements. Here we come back to Freud's early statement that psychoneuroses are really not diseases in the strict medical sense of the word,[1] but arrests in the process of sexual adjustment. They represent attempts to overcome the birth trauma, although the attempts have failed. In cultural adjustment, with all its difficult normal and super-normal achievements, we witness various largely successful attempts to overcome the birth trauma, among the most successful of which we must reckon Psychoanalysis—and by no means only in its therapeutic application.

In the last resort, then, the neurosis problem reduces itself to one of *form*. For we see in the child's biological adjust-ment to the extrauterine situation, in the normal adjustment of civilized man, as well as in his compensatory super-productions of art (in the widest sense), the same striving to overcome the birth trauma enacted in similar forms, the only essential difference being that the *civilized human being* and still more the " *artist* " can *reproduce this objectively* in manifold, strictly determined forms, fixed by the primal trauma, whilst the *neurotic* is compelled again and again to *produce it in a similar way only on his own body*.[2] But the

---

[1] A statement which Jung could confirm for the psychoses, which, according to him, struggle with the same " complexes " which the normal individual has mastered.

[2] See Ferenczi's quotation of the Freudian conception of an autoplastic stage.

essence of most pathological processes seems to rest on this compulsive " return of the same " product on one's own body. The neurotic is thrown back again and again to the real birth trauma, whilst the normal and supernormal throw it, so to say, forwards and project it outwards, and are thus enabled to objectify it.

In conclusion we shall give a short account of the way in which we work therapeutically and in what the healing factor consists. Thus we have once more to accept analytic knowledge and the way to it, as something already given. Analysis is now in the position to free itself to an extensive degree from the work of investigation, since we know from the outset not only the whole content of the Unconscious and the psychical mechanisms, but also what for the time being is the final element, the primal trauma. As the patient as a rule begins with a transference, it is technically possible to begin with the disclosure of the primal trauma, instead of giving the patient time automatically to repeat it at the end of the analysis. By this method one is enabled to sever the Gordian knot of the primal repression with one powerful cut, instead of laboriously troubling to unknot it—a process which succeeds with great difficulty since every bit of unravelling on the one side draws the knots so much the more tightly together on the other. After the disclosure of its foundation the reconstruction of childhood history proceeds without any trouble according to its clearly outlined plan, as it were, from its base upwards, whereby also memory, which was repressed with the primal trauma, appears on the scene. Thus it is a matter of allowing the patient, who in his neurosis has fled back to the mother fixation, *to repeat and to understand the birth trauma and its solution during the analysis in the transference*, without allowing him the unconscious reproduction of the same in the severance from the analyst. The enormous therapeutic advantage which one attains through the disclosure of the primal fixation at the right time is that, at the end of the analysis, instead of the reproduction of the birth trauma one can obtain in a pure form the sexual conflicts from which the patient has fled (Œdipus complex, etc.) and the guilt feeling (instead of anxiety) belonging to them; and thus one can solve them undisturbed by the regression mechanism. The means to this end is the identification with the analyst following from the transference. Through the libidinal element in the identification the patient learns to overcome anxiety through the sexual side of the transference. Thus, finally, in therapy the compulsion to the repetition (repro- duction) of the primal trauma or of the primal situation is removed, in that the direction of the libido is changed in the sense of striving for adjustment.

All this results by means of the technique of association and of interpretation, developed by Freud, whereby we use our own Unconscious as the main way leading to the patient's Unconscious.[1] This is the only means by which we can operate on his libido. In this way we allow him, so to speak, temporarily, a far-reaching restoration of the primal situation, in that we urge his Unconscious to it by " privation " (Freud), in order then immediately to convince his conscious Ego of the impossibility and objectionableness of this aim; we show up the infantile character of this tendency instead of allowing it to be discouraged through continuous productions of anxiety. The most important technical means, the severance from the substitute object of the libido, the analyst, is not merely employed at the height

[1] Freud's comparison of *the receiver* (*Coll. Papers*, vol. ii., p. 328).

of the unfolding of the transference by the irrevocable fixing of the termination, but it comes into action quite automatically from the beginning. Not only is the patient always conscious that the cure must one day be finished, but every single hour demands from him the repetition in miniature of the fixation and severance, till he is in the position finally to carry it through. In addition, the analyst is placed before him as the master to the pupil, and the patient, like the pupil, can only learn by identifying himself with the teacher, that is, by accepting the attitude of the analyst to the Unconscious and by taking him as an Ego-ideal. This brings us up against the problem of the father transference, the importance of which for analytic technique is justified by its therapeutic function. The patient must learn in the course of the analysis so far to solve the primal repression, clinging to the mother, through " transference " that he is able to transfer it to a real substitute object, without taking with it the primal repression. This attempt, which occurs automatically in normal development with more or less success, the neurotic, by the aid of conscious forces, has to make in the analysis, in which, by every means of making conscious his unconscious regressive tendencies, we appeal to his conscious Ego in order to strengthen it against the overpowerful Unconscious.

We notice in this process that the patient has finally nothing else to do than to supplement a part of his development which was neglected or lacking (what Freud calls re-education). And the part in question is that stage of social and human development which, on the one hand is made necessary and, on the other hand, is rendered more difficult by the birth trauma, namely, detachment from the mother fixation by transference of the libido to the father

(Bachofen's " masculine principle "). Analytically expressed, this is the phase *before* the development of the Œdipus complex. Against this re-education the Unconscious of the patient defends itself by means of libido resistance, by desiring the full maternal libido gratification from the analyst, whether it is in the heterosexual or homosexual repetition of the Œdipus situation. That his Ego is in the position, through identification with the analyst, to overcome in the transference these actual libidinal tendencies as well as the regressive maternal tendencies, can be explained from the fact that his Ego from the very beginning was created and developed from the Unconscious for this special task. In analysis this normal means of help to development is then finally strengthened through conscious modification, and the fact of his identification with the analyst is ultimately made conscious to the patient, thereby making him independent of the analyst.

If in the end we have to turn to so weak a thing as consciousness for support, we may yet console ourselves with the following reflections. Though consciousness is but a feeble weapon, it is the only one accessible to us in the fight against neurosis. The psychical anchoring in consciousness of the anxiety perception at parturition acts biologically as a therapeutic means against the backward striving tendency, and determines, as we have attempted to show, the actual process of becoming a human being. And consciousness is the human characteristic *par excellence*. Should not then the removal, by analysis, of the primal repression and its anchoring in consciousness be sufficient to make the neurotic grow up to the same limited degree as that reached by the ordinary civilized human being, who even today is only in the " short clothes " stage ? For the neurotic has only remained fixed in the birth trauma a little earlier than most people, and all we can ask of Psychotherapy is that it should bring him up to the " short clothes " stage, at which the bulk of humanity has remained to this day.

INDEX

Lightning Source UK Ltd.
Milton Keynes UK
UKHW011318230620
365452UK00001B/144